KEYS TO CHINESE CHARACTER W

Keys to
Chinese Character Writing
漢字入門

By Jing-Heng Sheng Ma

馬盛靜恆 著

The Chinese University Press

Keys to Chinese Character Writing
  By Jing-Heng Sheng Ma

© **The Chinese University of Hong Kong**, 2006

ISBN 962–996–292–6

THE CHINESE UNIVERSITY PRESS
The Chinese University of Hong Kong
SHA TIN, N.T., HONG KONG
Fax: +852 2603 6692
      +852 2603 7355
E-mail: cup@cuhk.edu.hk
Web-site: www.chineseupress.com

Printed in Hong Kong

Contents

Preface vii

Acknowledgements ix

Introduction xi

Part 1   Lessons and Worksheets on Strokes and Stroke Order

Strokes and Stroke Order Lesson 1 3

Strokes and Stroke Order Worksheet 1 6

Strokes and Stroke Order Lesson 2 11

Strokes and Stroke Order Worksheet 2 14

Strokes and Stroke Order Lesson 3 19

Strokes and Stroke Order Worksheet 3 23

Strokes and Stroke Order Lesson 4 27

Strokes and Stroke Order Worksheet 4 30

Strokes and Stroke Order Lesson 5 35

Strokes and Stroke Order Worksheet 5 38

Strokes and Stroke Order Lesson 6 43

Strokes and Stroke Order Worksheet 6 46

Strokes and Stroke Order Lesson 7 50

Strokes and Stroke Order Worksheet 7 53

Part 2   Lessons on the 18 Most Frequently-used Radicals

Radical Lesson 1 : 人 / 亻 (single man) 59

Radical Lesson 2 : 口 (mouth) 63

Radical Lesson 3 : 土 / 土 (earth) 66

Radical Lesson 4 : 女 (woman) 69

Radical Lesson 5 : 彳 (double man) 72

Radical Lesson 6 : 心 / 忄 (heart) 75

Radical Lesson 7 : 手 / 扌 (hand) 78

Radical Lesson 8 : 日 (sun) 81

Radical Lesson 9 : 木 (wood) 84

Radical Lesson 10: 水 / 氵 (water) 88

Radical Lesson 11: 火 / 灬 (fire) 92

Radical Lesson 12: 竹 / 竹 (bamboo) 96

Radical Lesson 13: 糸 / 纟 (silk) 100

Radical Lesson 14: 艸 / 艹 (grass) 104

Radical Lesson 15: 言 (speech) 108

Radical Lesson 16: 足 / 𧾷 (foot)   113

Radical Lesson 17: 辵 / 辶 (go, run)   117

Radical Lesson 18: 金 / 釒 (gold)   122

Part 3   Quizzes on Strokes and Stroke Order / Radicals

Quiz 1 (Strokes and Stroke Order Lessons 1–3)   129

Quiz 2 (Strokes and Stroke Order Lessons 4–5)   132

Quiz 3 (Strokes and Stroke Order Lessons 6–7)   135

Quiz 4 (Radical Lessons 1–3)   138

Quiz 5 (Radical Lessons 4–6)   140

Quiz 6 (Radical Lessons 7–9)   143

Quiz 7 (Radical Lessons 10–12)   146

Quiz 8 (Radical Lessons 13–15)   149

Quiz 9 (Radical Lessons 16–18)   153

Part 4   Answer Keys for Radical Lessons / Quizzes

Answer Keys for Radical Lessons   159

Answer Keys for Quizzes   164

Appendixes

Index: Strokes and Stroke Order Lessons   173

Index: Radical Lessons   177

Flash Cards for Strokes and Stroke Order Lessons   183

Flash Cards for Radical Lessons   185

79 Common Chinese Radicals   191

Preface

· · · · · · · ·

The most interesting and challenging aspect of studying Chinese is writing Chinese characters. Even though Chinese characters are one of the most distinctive features of the Chinese language, they often receive only marginal attention in the classroom. There are literally thousands of characters that a student must learn if he or she expects to be literate in the language. Given that the words taught in current Chinese language textbooks are based on the spoken language rather than the principles of character formation, and given the pressure of class time to deal with spoken competencies, the teaching of Chinese characters is rarely presented to students in a systematic way. Learners are left to find their own way as they memorize character by character, making mistakes in orthography without really understanding why. Furthermore, since Chinese characters are basically derivatives of pictorial representations of things and ideas and do not directly represent pronunciation, beginners must learn an entirely separate system of strokes and components that bear no relation to the spoken aspects of the language.

Keys to Chinese Character Writing is a self-paced learning pack. It is designed to address the common problems that beginners face when learning the orthography of Chinese characters (Hànzì). It offers systematic instruction in writing Hànzì. Through this learning pack, one will learn the principles that govern the construction of Hànzì — the basic strokes (bǐhuà) that comprise Hànzì, and the proper stroke order (bǐshùn) used to write Hànzì. Learning the proper stroke order will make writing Hànzì not only faster, but also more accurate. One will also learn the most frequently-used radicals (bùshǒu) for looking up words in a dictionary. More importantly, knowing bùshǒu can make the task of learning written Chinese much easier because they are parts of the elements that make up Hànzì. For example, the bùshǒu "shuǐ" (水/氵; water) appears in words related to water:

河	酒	流	渴
hé	jiǔ	liú	kě
river	wine	flow	thirsty

79 frequently-used bùshǒu are listed in the appendix; some can stand as independent characters as well as serving as parts of other characters, others are seldom or never used independently. The 18 most frequently-used bùshǒu are marked in the appendix with an asterisk (*). More than 50% of Chinese characters are based on one or another of these bùshǒu. In each example given, the shaded strokes indicate which bùshǒu is being discussed.

Keys to Chinese Character Writing has two components in total: the textbook and the

DVD. Each component can be used independently, but using them together proves to be more effective and more enjoyable for learning the Chinese writing system. This learning pack contains 25 lessons, seven of which are on bǐhuà and bǐshùn[1], and the rest are on bùshǒu. Each lesson introduces five Hànzì. 11 basic strokes and 35 Hànzì have been chosen for practice in the Strokes and Stroke Order lessons. 90 Hànzì have been chosen for practice in the Radical lessons. Through this learning pack, one can learn 125 Hànzì and some of the common words and phrases in which they are used, thus enabling them to build their writing repertoire at a faster pace.

In order to help learners revise and use the Hànzì that they have learned in a meaningful context, different writing drills and nine quizzes are designed for self-assessment. Learners are encouraged to work on them. Answer keys are included in the book. Flash cards for the 125 Hànzì introduced in this learning pack are also provided for students to do revision.

The most effective way to use this learning pack is to view the DVD prior to writing the characters on the textbook. This pack is designed for beginners to learn one or two lessons per day. The DVD shows the Hànzì being written by a calligrapher while the Hànzì are pronounced by a native speaker, with the meanings of the Hànzì illustrated on the screen.

This learning pack presents Hànzì in the "traditional" form as opposed to the "simplified" form. Learners will eventually have to learn both forms. Many years of teaching experience indicate that it is easier for learners to start with the traditional form of written Chinese. The pīnyīn of each Hànzì introduced in the book is included to assist learners with the pronunciation. The four tone markers used with pīnyīn are ‾ for the first tone, ´ for the second tone, ˇ for the third tone, ˋ for the fourth tone, and no tone marker for the unstressed neutral tone.

Keys to Chinese Character Writing is designed for beginners of Chinese. Intermediate learners who wish to learn the most effective way of writing Hànzì will also find this learning pack useful. The pack can be used prior to any elementary Chinese language textbook too.

---

[1] The bǐshùn of some characters may vary. The bǐshùn of this book is based on the *Changyongzi Biaozhun Ziti Bishun Shouce* (Handbook of Stroke Order for Commonly Used National Standard Characters). Taipei: Taiwan Ministry of Education, 1996.

Acknowledgements

This project was generously funded by a special gift contributed by Mrs. Elizabeth Tu Hoffman. I would like to express my deepest appreciation for their support and encouragement.

This project could not succeed without institutional support and the help of many people. I would like to thank Wellesley College for the wonderful technology resources provided; Kenneth B. Freundlich, Manager Advisor Technology Applications, and Jarlath Waldron, Co-Director of Knapp Media and Technology Center, for their excellent technical support and advice; and Caroline S. Tsai and Yelena Nakhmovsky, students of Wellesley College, for their technological skills and many hours of recording, videotaping, and editing of the videotape. I wish to thank my colleagues Dai Chen, Ruby Lam, and Weina Zhao for their warm friendship, support, and valuable suggestions. My thank also goes to my students at Wellesley College, who have used this material and given feedback that has helped me to improve this learning pack. I am very grateful to Robert H. Smitheram, Advisor of Courserware Development & Instructional Technology at Middlebury College, for his willingness to develop the computer software for this project.

Special gratitude goes to Professor Cornelius C. Kubler, of Williams College, for his generous critique of the pedagogical principles employed; to my dear friends, Professor Irwin and Mrs. Helene Schulman, for their many valuable comments and editorial suggestions; and to my husband, Wei-yi Ma, for his beautiful calligraphy used in this learning pack.

Introduction

The Chinese Writing System

Some 4,000 years ago, Chinese was not yet a written language. A handful of characters had been invented, mostly for ritual purposes, to be inscribed on bronze vessels and oracle bones. As Chinese civilization developed, giving rise to officials, traders, poets, and scholars, more and more characters had to be invented in order to record, circulate, read and preserve our daily experiences in forms of documents, books, poems, and letters. Because Chinese is a living language, this process of creating and revising characters has been continuing throughout the years. By the Ming dynasty (1368–1644) there were thousands of characters in use. The Kāngxī Zìdiǎn, published about 300 years ago, identified some 40,000 different characters.

Chinese characters were classified into six categories by Xǔ Shèn of the Eastern Han period (25–220). These six categories were based on six methods of character formation: xiàngxíng (象形; pictographs), zhǐshì (指事; ideograph), huìyì (會意; logical compounds), jiǎjiè (假借; phonetic borrowings), xíngshēng (形聲; phonetic compounds), and zhuǎnzhù (轉注; semantic extensions).[1]

Pictograph is the simplest and the smallest group, it contains characters descended directly from ancient pictorial writing, such as the ones shown below:

Ancient form	Modern form	Definition
⊙	日 rì	sun: a depiction of the sun
夕	月 yuè	moon or month: a depiction of the moon
⋀	山 shān	mountain: a depiction of mountain peaks
▽	口 kǒu	mouth: a depiction of an open mouth

Ideograph uses symbols to indicate abstract meanings. A few examples of ideographs are as follows:

---

[1] Xíngshēng and zhuǎnzhù are in fact methods of expanding the vocabulary pool; we will not discuss them in this introduction.

Ancient form	Modern form	Definition
⌣	上 shàng	above: the long curve indicates a border, above which sits a dot
⌢	下 xià	below: the long curve indicates a border, below which sits a dot
──	一 yī	one: one stroke
──	二 èr	two: two strokes

The Logical Compound method of creating characters combines two or more ideographic symbols to form a new character. When putting the characters 日 rì "sun" and 月 yuè "moon" side by side, another character 明 míng "bright" is formed. When placing the character 木 mù "tree" next to another 木, another character 林 lín "woods" is formed.

The Phonetic Compound method of creating characters uses the combination of a radical (or indicator of meaning) and a phonetic part (or clue to pronunciation) to construct a character. For example, the character 瘋 fēng "crazy, insane," is made up of a phonetic part 風 fēng written inside the radical 疒 for disease. This method makes it possible to create large numbers of new characters to express all kinds of concepts. Today, more than 90% of Chinese characters in use are phonetic compounds.

As characters proliferated, Chinese scholars recognized the need for some rules to govern the invention of new characters, and for a method of classifying and indexing the characters already in use. Certain symbols recur in character after character, often revealing or suggesting meaning. These symbols are called radicals (bùshǒu).

In the Ming dynasty, scholars agreed on a system of 214 radicals that are still in use today. Dictionaries are organized by radicals, in a standard sequence based on the number of strokes of a radical. In the beginning of every dictionary are all those characters with one-stroke radicals; and at the end are all those characters based on the 214th radical, which has 17 strokes. Under each radical the characters are presented according to the number of strokes in the other part, in ascending order. It is not a perfect system: often the radical has only the slightest bearing on the character's meaning; some radicals have one or more variant forms. Indeed, the 214 radicals can be written in a total of 258 forms: 36 radicals have alternate forms, and eight of them can be written three different ways.

The writing of Chinese became standardized, particularly for the purpose of creating government documents and printing books, some 2,000 years ago. Over the centuries, the standard form has changed little. In the 1950s, the People's Republic of China began to promote the use of "simplified" characters as part of an effort to increase literacy in China.

Bǐhuà 筆劃 (Strokes)

Chinese characters are composed of various strokes, and their structures may seem very complicated to a beginner. In fact, the various strokes one encounters in written or printed Chinese fall into a fairly limited number of forms. These stroke forms are described below. For each stroke form, an example of a character using that form is presented. In each example, the shaded stroke is the one being illustrated, and the arrow shows the direction followed by the pen (or brush) when writing that stroke.

✎ (1) Héng 橫 (Horizontal stroke)

The horizontal stroke can be either short or long. The stroke is written from left to right, but never the other way around.

✎ (2) Shù 豎 (Vertical stroke)

Always write the vertical stroke from the top downward.

✎ (3) Piě 撇 (Left-falling stroke)

The left-falling stroke is used in different lengths and angles, but all are only variations on the basic way of writing the stroke. Write the stroke from top right to bottom left.

✎ (4) Nà 捺 (Right-falling stroke)

There are two forms of the right-falling stroke: slanted and flat. Write the stroke from top left to bottom right.

✎ (5) Diǎn 點 (Dot)

The dot takes many forms, as illustrated below:

✎ (6) Gōu 鉤 (Hook)

There are four forms of hook. Pay attention to the direction that the stroke takes in different forms.

Shù gōu (Standing hook)   Héng gōu (Flat hook)

Xié gōu (Slanted hook)   Wò gōu (Sleeping hook)

✎ (7) Zhé 折 (Angle stroke)

There are three forms of angle stroke. Pay attention to the direction that the stroke takes in different forms.

Héng zhé (Horizontal angle)   Shù zhé (Vertical angle)

Xié zhé (Slanted angle)

✎ (8) Tí 提 (Left-rising stroke)

There are two forms of left-rising stroke. Write the left-rising stroke from bottom left to top right.

✎ (9) Zhé gōu 折鈎 (Curved hook)

There are three forms of curved hook. Pay attention to the direction that the stroke takes in different forms.

Shù zhé gōu (Vertical curved hook)   **Héng shù gōu** (curved hook)

Héng zhē gōu (Horizontal curved hook)

✎ (10) Héng zhé piě 橫折撇 (Horizontal angle, left-falling stroke)

There are two types of horizontal angle, left-falling stroke, short and long, as illustrated below:

✎ (11) Héng piě wān gōu 橫撇彎鈎 (Double-curved hook)

Pay attention to this stroke. It is different from the stroke héng zhé piě as illustrated in (10).

Bǐshùn 筆順 (Stroke Order):

Each Chinese character contains a certain number of strokes and they must be written in a proper order. The misplacement of a stroke can sometimes completely alter the meaning of a word, causing confusion. Below are the ten basic rules of stroke order for the writing of Chinese characters.

Rule	Example	Stroke Order
✎ (1) First héng (一), then shù (丨).	十	十 十
✎ (2) First piě (丿), then nà (乀).	人	人 人
✎ (3) First top, then bottom.	二	二 二
✎ (4) First left, then right.	你	你 你
✎ (5) First outside, then inside.	月	月 月
✎ (6) First inside, then the sealing stroke.	日	日 日
✎ (7) First center, then sides.	小	小 小
✎ (8) First horizontal, then piě (丿), and then nà (乀).	大	大 大

✎ (9) First the main body, then the middle.

✎ (10) For characters with special stroke order:

(A) Write the diǎn (、) last if it is positioned at the top right corner of a character.

(B) Write the diǎn (、) last if it is positioned inside a character or a component.

(C) If a character is made up of the component 辶 or 廴 with some other component(s), write the 辶 or 廴 last (as sealing strokes), as illustrated below.

(D) If a character consists of only a few hēng (一) and shù (丨), write the shù first, and the hēng at the bottom last.

(E) If a character has a hēng (一) in the middle, write the hēng last, as illustrated below.

女　女　女

冊　冊　冊

PART *1*

· · · · · · · · · · · · · · · · ·

Lessons and Worksheets

on

Strokes and Stroke Order

Strokes and Stroke Order Lesson 1

1. Bǐhuà (Stroke)

✎ Héng (Horizontal stroke): Write from left to right.

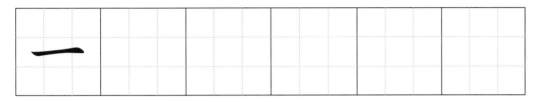

✎ Shù (Vertical stroke): Write from top to bottom.

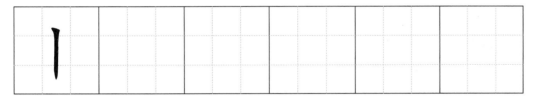

2. Hànzì (Chinese Characters)

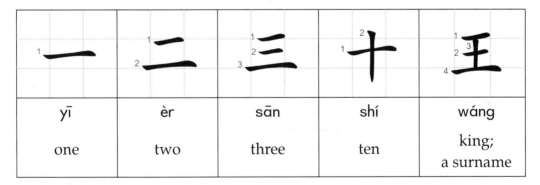

一	二	三	十	王
yī	èr	sān	shí	wáng
one	two	three	ten	king; a surname

3. Bǐshùn (Stroke Order)

✎ Write from left to right, then from top to bottom. Remember to start with the uppermost stroke.

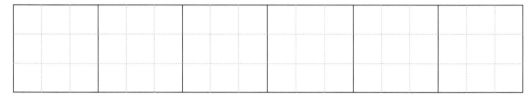

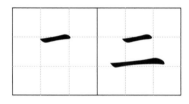

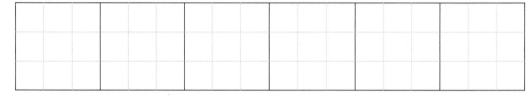

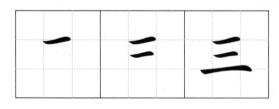

✎ Write héng first, then shù.

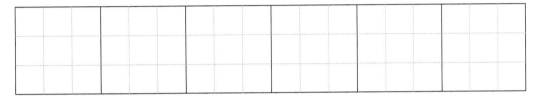

✎ Write the two uppermost héng first, then shù, and then the bottom héng.

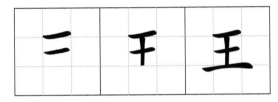

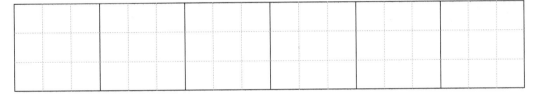

Strokes and Stroke Order Worksheet 1

I.   Write down the pīnyīn and the meaning of the following Hànzì. Then practice the Hànzì in the correct stroke order.

1.

Pīnyīn _____

Meaning _____

2.

Pīnyīn _____

Meaning _____

3.

Pīnyīn _____

Meaning _____

4.

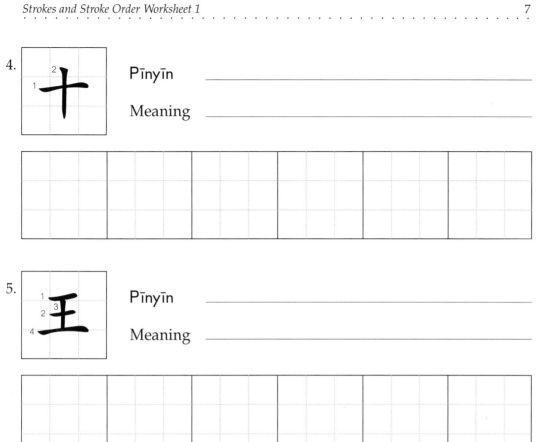

Pīnyīn _____

Meaning _____

5.

Pīnyīn _____

Meaning _____

II. Practice the following **Hànzì** and learn their meanings.

1.

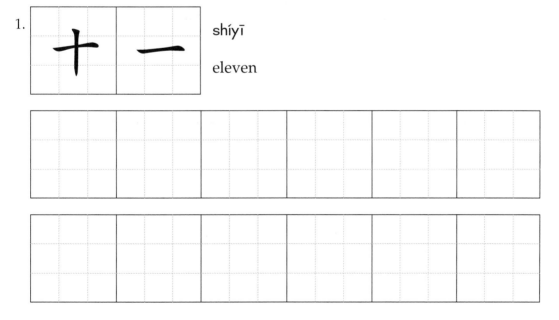

shíyī

eleven

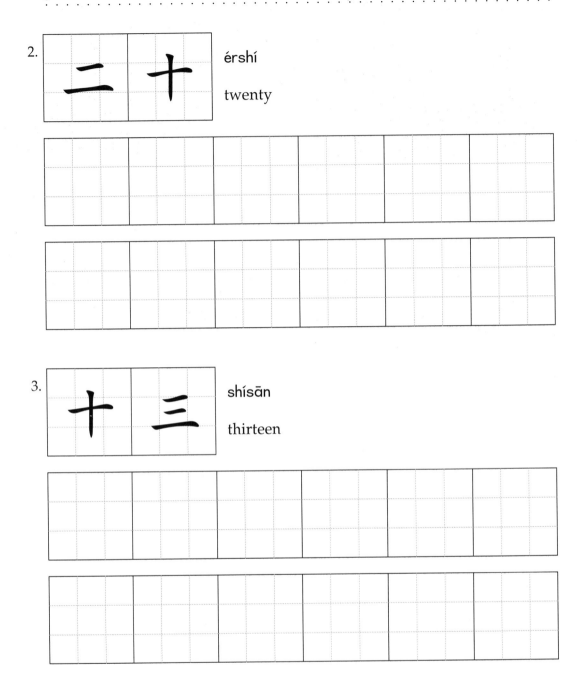

2. 二十 érshí
         twenty

3. 十三 shísān
         thirteen

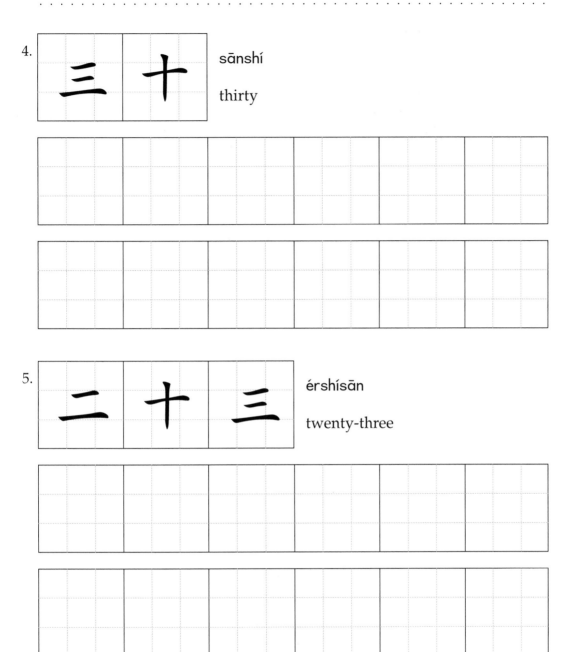

4. 三 十   sānshí

thirty

5. 二 十 三   érshísān

twenty-three

6.

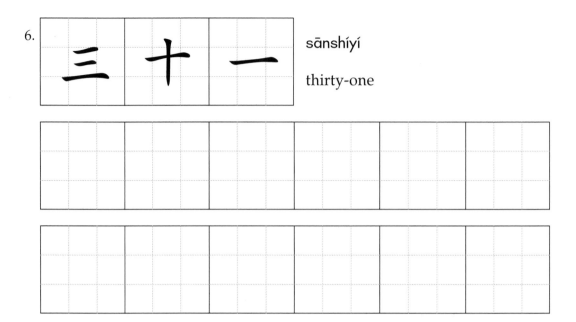

sānshíyí

thirty-one

Strokes and Stroke Order Lesson 2

1. Bǐhuà (Stroke)

✎ Piě (Left-falling stroke): Write a right to left diagonal, with slight curve.

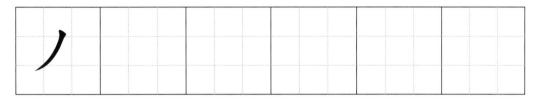

✎ Héng piě (Horizontal, then left-falling stroke): Write a héng, then a piě.

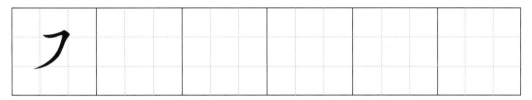

✎ Nà (Right-falling stroke): Write a left to right diagonal, with the end of the stroke flattened to the bottom.

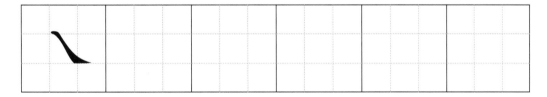

2. Hànzì (Chinese Characters)

人	八	大	天	又
rén	bā	dà	tiān	yòu
human being; person	eight	big	sky; day	again

3. Bǐshùn (Stroke Order)

✎ Write piě first, then nà.

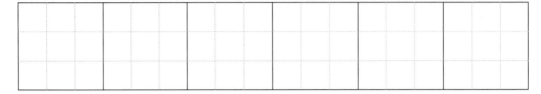

✎ Write héng first, then piě, and then nà.

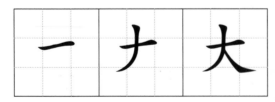

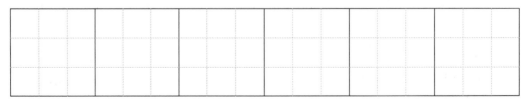

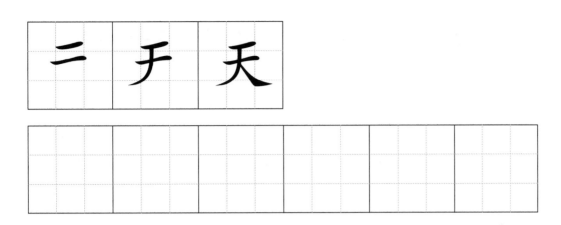

✏ Write héng piě first, then nà.

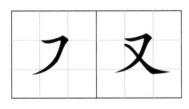

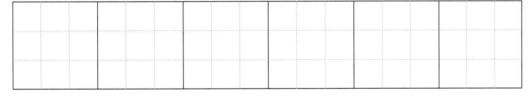

Strokes and Stroke Order Worksheet 2

I. Write down the pīnyīn and the meaning of the following Hànzì. Then practice the Hànzì in the correct stroke order.

1.
人

Pīnyīn _____

Meaning _____

2.
八

Pīnyīn _____

Meaning _____

3.
大

Pīnyīn _____

Meaning _____

4.   Pīnyīn _____

Meaning _____

5.   Pīnyīn _____

Meaning _____

II. Practice the following Hànzì and learn their meanings.

1.  dàrén

adult

2.

八　天

bā tiān

eight days

3.

十　天

shí tiān

ten days

4.

tiāntiān

every day, daily

5.

bāshí tiān

eighty days

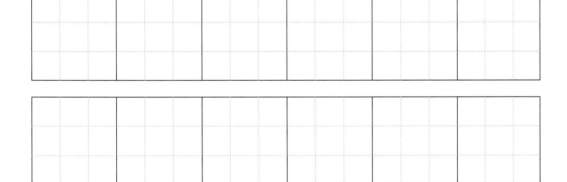

6.

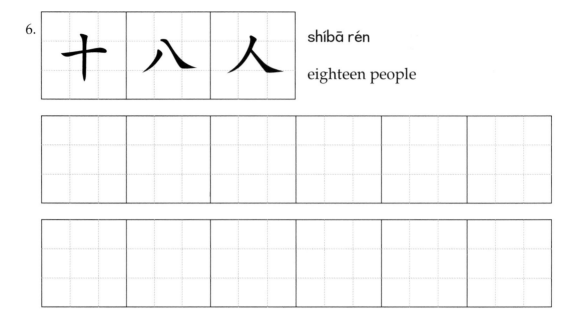

shíbā rén

eighteen people

Strokes and Stroke Order Lesson 3

1. Bǐhuà (Stroke)

✎ Diǎn (Dot):

- Write a tiny dash falling leftwards.

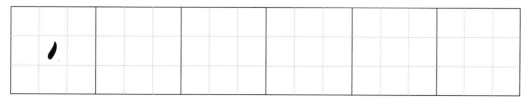

- Write a tiny dash falling rightwards.

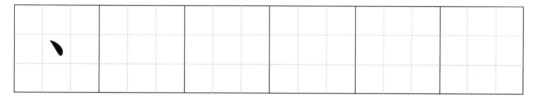

✎ Gōu (Hook):

- Shù gōu (Standing hook): Write a shù, then hook up to the left/right.

- **Héng gōu** (Flat hook): Write a héng, then hook back down to the left.

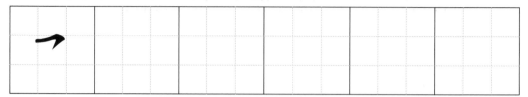

- **Xié gōu** (Slanted hook): Write a nà, then end the stroke with a hook.

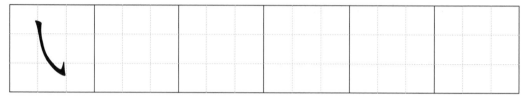

- **Wò gōu** (Sleeping hook): Write a straight line down that bends into a flat line going rightwards, then end the stroke with a hook.

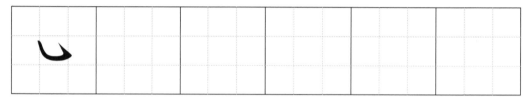

2. Hànzì (Chinese Characters)

小	長	你	我	心
xiǎo	cháng	nǐ	wǒ	xīn
small	long	you	I, me	heart; mind

3. Bǐshùn (Stroke Order)

✎ Write shù in the center first, then the left-hand side diǎn, and then the right-hand side diǎn.

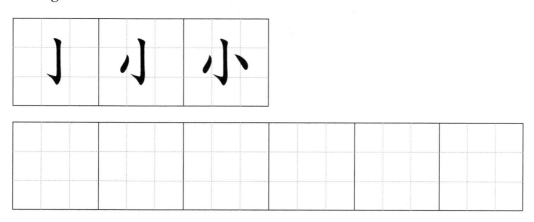

✎ Follow the "from left to right" and "from top to bottom" stroke orders.

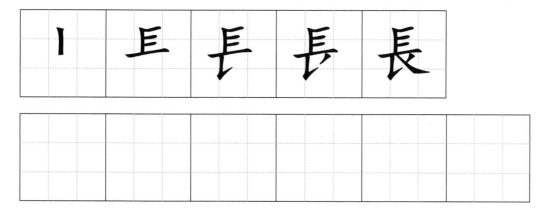

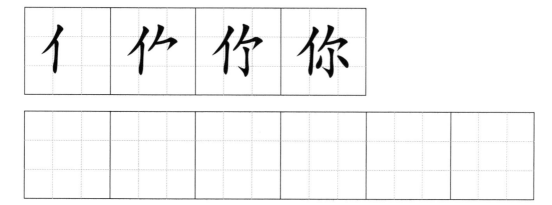

✎ Follow the "from left to right" and "from top to bottom" stroke orders.
Write the **diǎn** last.

✎ Follow the "from left to right" stroke order.

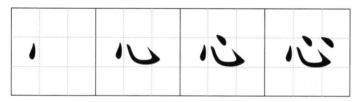

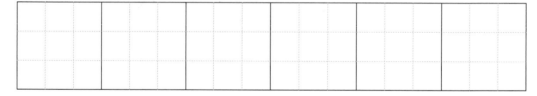

Strokes and Stroke Order Worksheet 3

I. Write down the pīnyīn and the meaning of the following Hànzì. Then practice the Hànzì in the correct stroke order.

1. 小

   Pīnyīn _____

   Meaning _____

2. 長

   Pīnyīn _____

   Meaning _____

3. 你

   Pīnyīn _____

   Meaning _____

4. 我

   Pīnyīn   _____

   Meaning   _____

5. 心

   Pīnyīn   _____

   Meaning   _____

II.   Practice the following **Hànzì** and learn their meanings.

1. 小 心

   Xiǎoxīn!

   Be careful; take care!

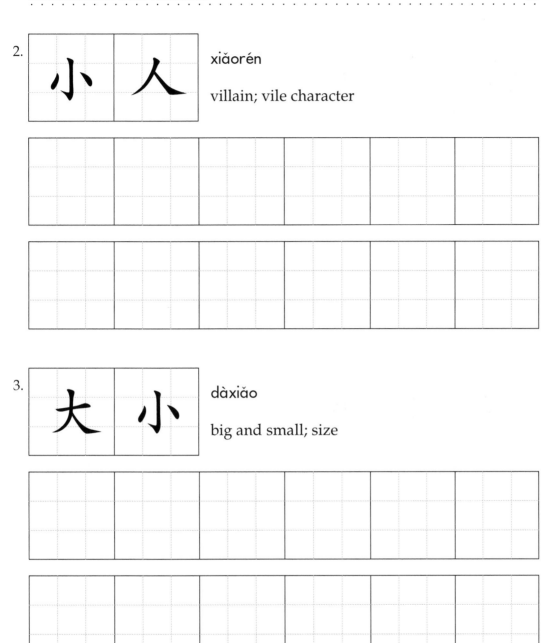

2. 小 人

xiǎorén

villain; vile character

3. 大 小

dàxiǎo

big and small; size

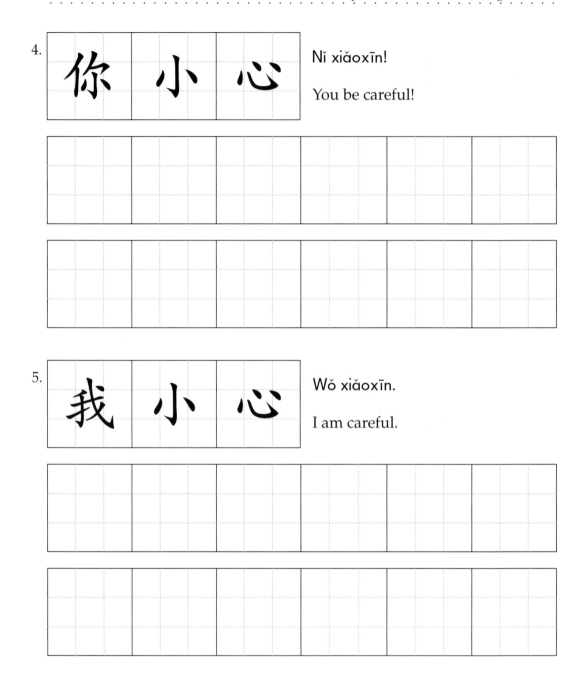

4. 你 小 心   Nǐ xiǎoxīn!

    You be careful!

5. 我 小 心   Wǒ xiǎoxīn.

    I am careful.

Go to Quiz 1 (Strokes and Stroke Order Lessons 1–3) on pages 129–31.

Strokes and Stroke Order Lesson 4

1. Bǐhuà (Stroke)

✎ Zhé (Angle stroke):

- Héng zhé (Horizontal angle): Write a héng, then turn downwards to form a shù.

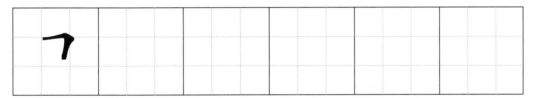

- Shù zhé (Vertical angle): Write a shù, then turn rightwards to form a héng.

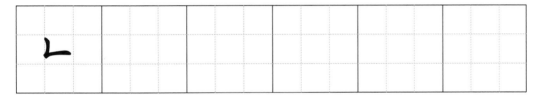

- Xié zhé (Slanted angle): Write a piě, then turn to the right.

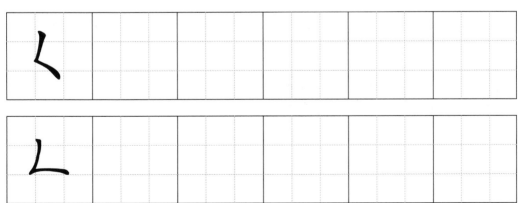

2. Hànzì (Chinese Characters)

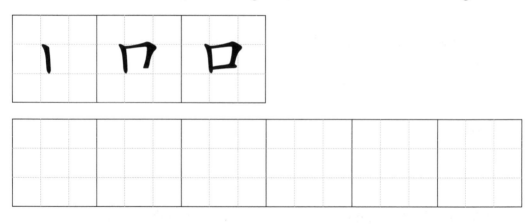

口	忙	女	要	去
kǒu	máng	nǚ	yào	qù
mouth	busy	female	want	go

3. Bǐshùn (Stroke Order)

✎ Write the left **shù** first, then **héng zhé**, and then the bottom **héng**.

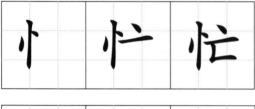

✎ Follow the "from left to right" and "from top to bottom" stroke orders.

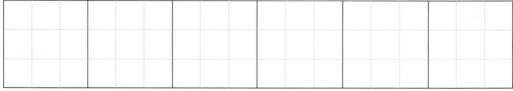

✎ Write **xié zhé** first, then **piě**, and then **héng**.

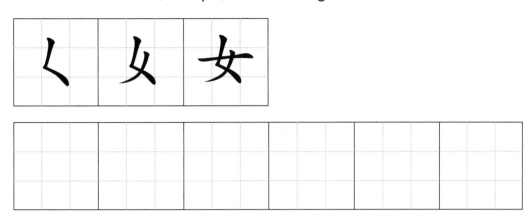

✎ Follow the "from top to bottom" stroke order first, then follow the stroke order of the word 女 (nǔ).

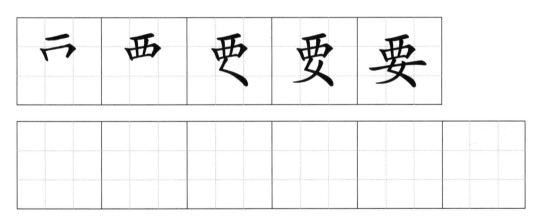

✎ Follow the "from top to bottom" and "from left to right" stroke orders.

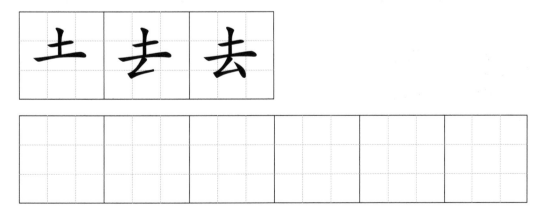

Strokes and Stroke Order Worksheet 4

I. Write down the pīnyīn and the meaning of the following Hànzì. Then practice the Hànzì in the correct stroke order.

1.

口

Pīnyīn _____

Meaning _____

2.

忙

Pīnyīn _____

Meaning _____

3.

女

Pīnyīn _____

Meaning _____

4. 要

Pīnyīn _____

Meaning _____

5. 去

Pīnyīn _____

Meaning _____

II. Practice the following **Hànzì** and learn their meanings.

1. 人 口

rénkǒu

population

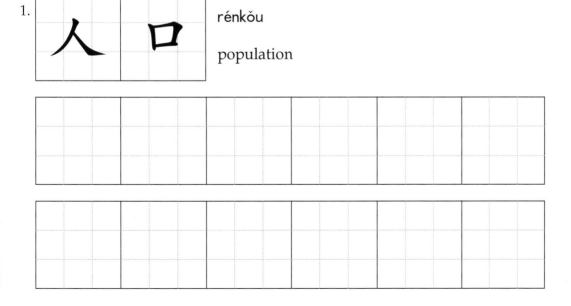

2.

入口

rùkǒu

entrance

3.

女人

nǚrén

woman, women

4.

你 去

Nǐ qù!

You go!

5.

我 忙

Wǒ máng.

I am busy.

6.

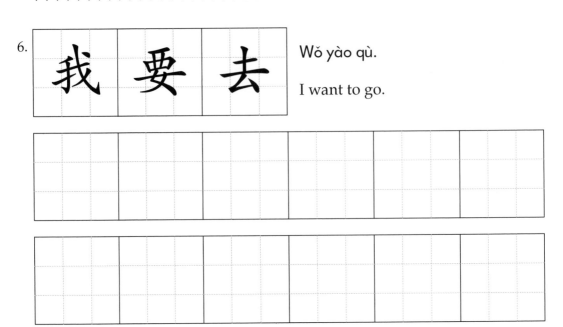

Wǒ yào qù.

I want to go.

Strokes and Stroke Order Lesson 5

1. Bǐhuà (Stroke)

✎ Tí (Left-rising stroke): Flick up the stroke to the right.

✓					

2. Hànzì (Chinese Characters)

冷	河	球	打	班
lěng	hé	qiú	dǎ	bān
cold	river	ball	hit; play	class

3. Bǐshùn (Stroke Order)

✎ Follow the "from left to right" and "from top to bottom" stroke orders.

冫	氵	冷

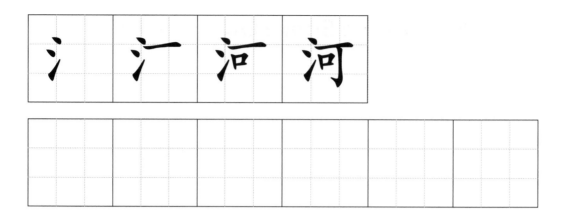

✎ Follow the "from left to right" and "héng first, then shù" stroke orders. Write the diǎn last.

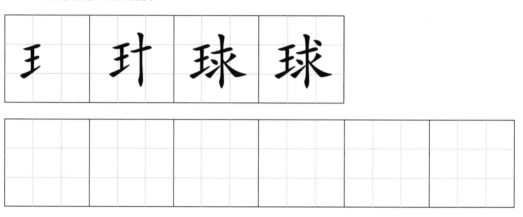

✎ Follow the "from left to right" and "héng first, then shù" stroke orders.

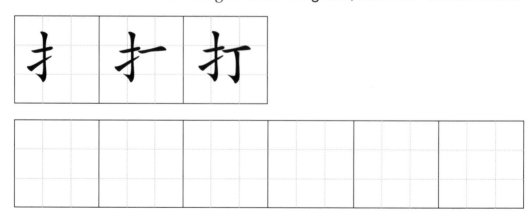

✎ Follow the "from left to right" and "from top to bottom" stroke orders.

Strokes and Stroke Order Worksheet 5

I. Write down the pīnyīn and the meaning of the following Hànzì. Then practice the Hànzì in the correct stroke order.

1. 冷   Pīnyīn _____

     Meaning _____

2. 河   Pīnyīn _____

     Meaning _____

3. 球   Pīnyīn _____

     Meaning _____

4.
打

Pīnyīn _____

Meaning _____

5.
班

Pīnyīn _____

Meaning _____

II. Practice the following Hànzì and learn their meanings.

1.
大 河

dà hé

big river

2.

大 班   dà bān

big class

3.

小 班   xiǎo bān

small class

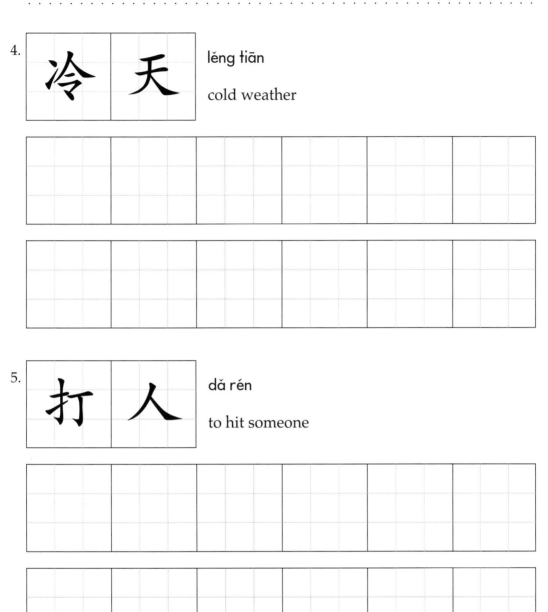

4. 冷天　lěng tiān
cold weather

5. 打人　dǎ rén
to hit someone

6.

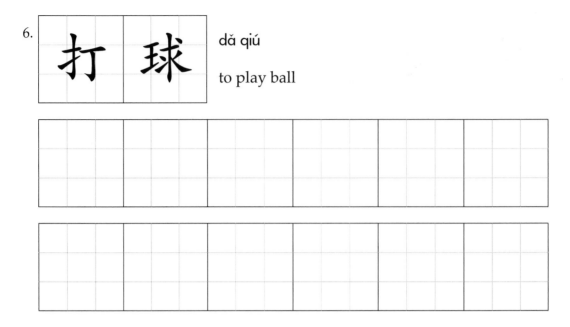

dǎ qiú

to play ball

Go to Quiz 2 (Strokes and Stroke Order Lessons 4–5) on pages 132–34.

Strokes and Stroke Order Lesson 6

1. Bǐhuà (Stroke)

✎ Zhé gōu (Curved hook):

- Shù zhé gōu (Vertical curved hook): Write a **shù zhé**, then hook up.

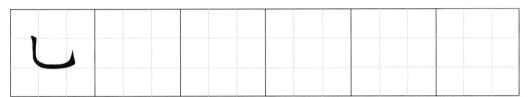

- Héng shù gōu (curved hook): Write a **héng**, then a **shù gōu**.

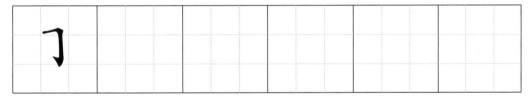

- Héng zhé gōu (Horizontal curved hook): Write a **héng zhé**, then hook up.

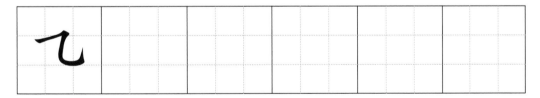

2. Hànzì (Chinese Characters)

也	有	九	吃	嗎
yě	yǒu	jiǔ	chī	ma
also	have	nine	to eat	(question marker)

3. Bǐshùn (Stroke Order)

✎ Write héng shù gōu first, then shù, and then shù zhé gōu.

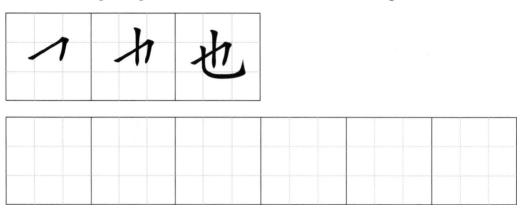

✎ Follow the "héng first, then piě" and "from left to right" stroke orders. Write the inside bottom héng last.

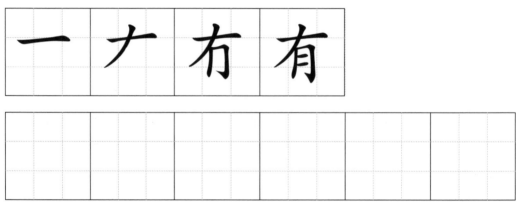

✎ Write piě, then héng zhé gōu.

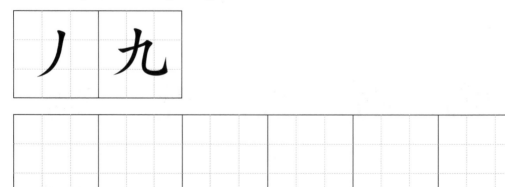

✎ Follow the "from left to right" and "from top to bottom" stroke orders.

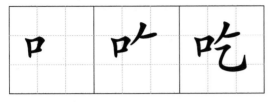

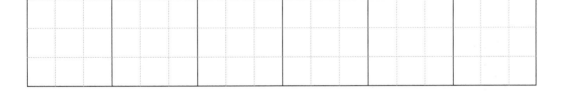

Strokes and Stroke Order Worksheet 6

I. Write down the pīnyīn and the meaning of the following Hànzì. Then practice the Hànzì in the correct stroke order.

1. 也

    Pīnyīn _____

    Meaning _____

2. 有

    Pīnyīn _____

    Meaning _____

3. 九

    Pīnyīn _____

    Meaning _____

4. 吃

Pīnyīn   _____

Meaning   _____

5. 嗎

Pīnyīn   _____

Meaning   _____

II. Practice the following **Hànzì** and learn their meanings.

1. 十九

shíjiǔ

nineteen

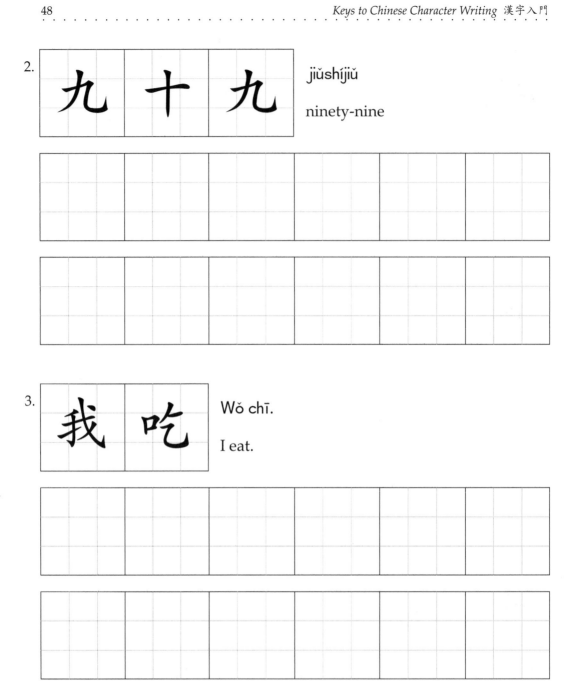

2. 九 十 九   jiǔshíjiǔ

ninety-nine

3. 我 吃   Wǒ chī.

I eat.

4.

| 你 | 也 | 吃 | 嗎 |

Nǐ yě chī ma?

Do you eat too?

5.

| 你 | 有 | 球 | 嗎 |

Nǐ yǒu qiú ma?

Do you have a ball?

Strokes and Stroke Order Lesson 7

1. Bǐhuà (Stroke)

✎ Héng zhé piě (Horizontal angle, left-falling stroke): Write a tiny héng piě first, then write a bigger héng piě at its bottom.

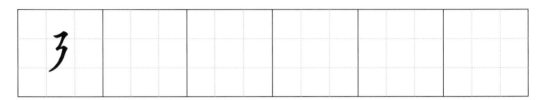

✎ Héng piě wān gōu (Double-curved hook): Write a héng piě first, then bend down the stroke a bit, and then hook it up to the left.

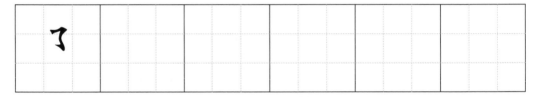

2. Hànzì (Chinese Characters)

建	這	那	都	院
jiàn	zhè/zhèi	nà/nèi	dōu	yuàn
to build	this	that	all	courtyard, yard

3. Bǐshùn (Stroke Order)

✎ Always write the bottom sealing stroke last. Write **héng zhé piě** first, then **nà**.

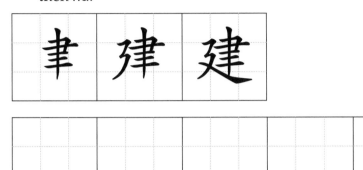

✎ Follow the "from top to bottom" stroke order. Always write the bottom sealing stroke last.

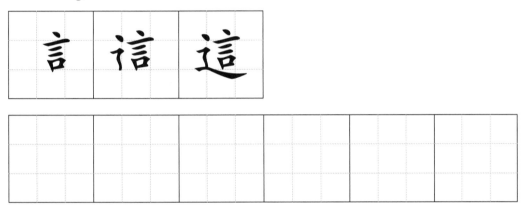

✎ Follow the "from left to right" stroke order. Write **héng piě wān gōu** first, and then **shù**.

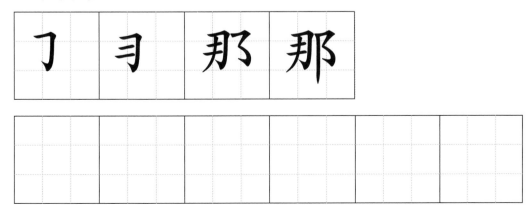

Strokes and Stroke Order Worksheet 7

I. Write down the pīnyīn and the meaning of the following Hànzì. Then practice the Hànzì in the correct stroke order.

1. 建

   Pīnyīn _____

   Meaning _____

2. 這

   Pīnyīn _____

   Meaning _____

3. 那

   Pīnyīn _____

   Meaning _____

4. 都

Pīnyīn _____

Meaning _____

5. 院

Pīnyīn _____

Meaning _____

II.   Practice the following Hànzì and learn their meanings.

1. 那 人 要 去

Nà rén yào qù.

That person wants to go.

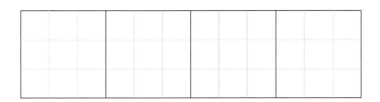

2.

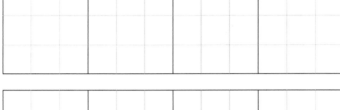

Zhè rén hǎo ma?

Is this person good?

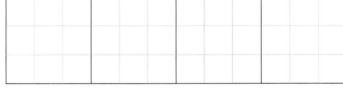

3.

Nà hé cháng ma?

Is that river long?

4.

Nǐ wǒ dōu máng.

Both you and I are busy.

Go to Quiz 3 (Strokes and Stroke Order Lessons 6–7) on pages 135–37.

PART 2

. . . .

Lessons on the 18 Most Frequently-used Radicals

Radical Lesson 1: 人 / 亻 (single man)

I. Circle the radical rén 人 / 亻 and write the following Hànzì according to the rules of bǐshùn.

1. 他 【tā】 he; she; him; her

2. 們 【men】 person (plural)

3. 今 【jīn】 modern; present-day

4.
太 【tài】 excessively, too; very

5.
來 【lái】 come; arrive

6.
我們 【wǒmen】 we; us

7.
你們 【nǐmen】 you (plural)

8.

他們 【tāmen】 they; them (plural)

9.

今天 【jīntiān】 today

10.

太太 【tàitai】 Mrs.; wife

11.

太大 【tài dà】 too big

II. Transcribe the following pīnyīn text into Hànzì, then give the English translation.

1. Q: Tāmen jīntiān lái ma?

   A: Lái.

   C Q: _____

       A: _____

   E Q: _____

       A: _____

2. Q: Wáng tàitai jīntiān lái ma?

   A: Tā yě lái.

   C Q: _____

       A: _____

   E Q: _____

       A: _____

➪ Please go to page 159 for the answer key.

Radical Lesson 2: 口 (mouth)

I. Circle the radical kǒu 口 and write the following Hànzi according to the rules of bǐshùn.

1.

喝

【hē】 drink

2.

問

【wèn】 ask, inquire

3.

哥

【gē】 elder brother

4.

【hé】 together with, and

5. 呢

【ne】 (question marker)

6. 哥哥

【gēge】 elder brother

II. Transcribe the following pīnyīn text into Hànzì, then give the English translation.

1. Tā yào qù wèn gēge. Nǐ ne?

C _____

_____

E _____

_____

2. Tā hé wǒ dōu yào qù wèn gēge.

C _____

_____

E _____

_____

3. Nǐ yào hē. Wǒ yǒ yào hē.

C _____

_____

E _____

_____

⇨ Please go to page 159 for the answer key.

Radical Lesson 3: 土 / 土 (earth)

I. Circle the radical tǔ 土 / 土 and write the following Hànzì according to the rules of bǐshùn.

1. 土 　【tǔ】 soil; earth

2. 地 　【dì】 earth; land; ground

3. 坐 　【zuò】 sit; take a seat; travel by (plane, train, etc.)

4.  【zài】 at; in; on; exist

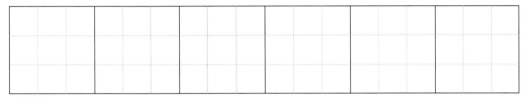

5. 報 【bào】 newspaper

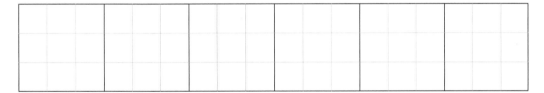

6. 土地 【tǔdì】 land

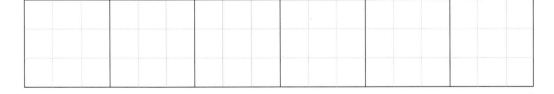

II. Transcribe the following pīnyīn text into Hànzì, then give the English translation.

1. Tāmen yǒu tǔdì ma?

C _____

_____

E _____

_____

2. Wǒmen zuò zài zhèr.

C _____

_____

E _____

_____

3. Q: Bào zài zhèr ma?

A: Zài.

C Q: _____

A: _____

E Q: _____

A: _____

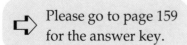
Please go to page 159 for the answer key.

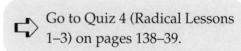
Go to Quiz 4 (Radical Lessons 1–3) on pages 138–39.

Radical Lesson 4: 女 (woman)

I. Circle the radical nǚ 女 and write the following Hànzì according to the rules of bǐshùn.

1. 媽

    【mā】 mom, mother

2. 姐

    【jiě】 elder sister

3. 妹

    【mèi】 younger sister

4.  好

【hǎo】 good, fine, nice; kind

5. 姓

【xìng】 surname, family name

6. 媽媽

【māma】 mom, mother

7. 姐姐

【jiějie】 elder sister

8.  **妹妹** 【mèimei】 younger sister

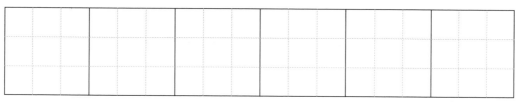

II. Transcribe the following pīnyīn text into Hànzì, then give the English translation.

1. Q: Nǐ jiějie, mèimei hǎo ma?

   A: Tāmen dōu hǎo.

   C Q: _____

   A: _____

   E Q: _____

   A: _____

2. Nǐ xìng Wáng. Wǒ yě xìng Wáng.

   C _____

   _____

   E _____

   _____

➡ Please go to page 159 for the answer key.

Radical Lesson 5: 彳 (double man)

I. Circle the radical **shuāng rén** 彳 and write the following Hànzì according to the rules of **bǐshùn**.

1. 很 【hěn】 very; quite; awfully

2. 後 【hòu】 back, behind, rear

3. 得 【děi】 need; must; have to

4.  【dài】 treat, deal with

5. 從 【cóng】 from

6. 後天 【hòutiān】 the day after tomorrow

II. Transcribe the following pīnyīn text into Hànzì, then give the English translation.

1. Wǒ hòutiān děi qù.

C _____

_____

E _____

_____

2. Wáng tàitai dài wǒ hěn hǎo.

C _____

_____

E _____

_____

3. Wǒ míngtiān děi cóng zhèr qù.

C _____

_____

E _____

_____

⇨ Please go to page 160 for the answer key.

Radical Lesson 6: 心 / 忄 (heart)

I. Circle the radical xīn 心 / 忄 and write the following Hànzì according to the rules of bǐshùn.

1. 想 【xiǎng】 think; suppose; consider; miss; would like to

2. 慢 【màn】 slow

3. 快 【kuài】 fast, quick; hurry up; soon

4.

【pà】 fear; dread; be afraid of

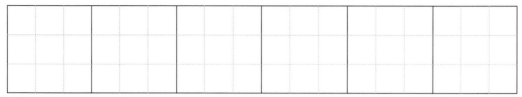

5.

【ài】 love, affection; like, be fond of

II. Transcribe the following pīnyīn text into Hànzì, then give the English translation.

1. Tāmen hěn xiǎng māma.

C _____

   _____

E _____

   _____

2. Nǐ mèimei pà gēge ma?

C _____

_____

E _____

_____

3. Nǐ tài kuài, wǒ tài màn.

C _____

_____

E _____

_____

4. Q: Nǐ ài wǒ ma?
   A: Ài.

C Q: _____

   A: _____

E Q: _____

   A: _____

 Please go to page 160 for the answer key.

 Go to Quiz 5 (Radical Lessons 4–6) on pages 140–42.

Radical Lesson 7: 手 / 扌 (hand)

I. Circle the radical shǒu 手 / 扌 and write the following Hànzì according to the rules of bǐshùn.

1.

【shǒu】 hand

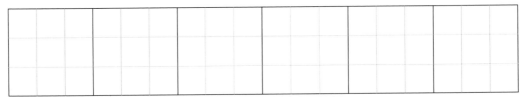

2. 指

【zhǐ】 finger; point at; point to

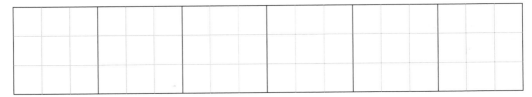

3. 找

【zhǎo】 look for, try to find; call on, ask for

4.

【ná】 hold; take; seize

5. 才

【cái】 just

6. 手心

【shǒuxīn】 palm

7. 手指

【shǒuzhǐ】 finger

II. Transcribe the following pīnyīn text into Hànzì, then give the English translation.

1. Wáng tàitai zhǎo nǐ.

C _____

_____

E _____

_____

2. Tā shǒuzhǐ hěn cháng.

C _____

_____

E _____

_____

3. Q: Wǒ míngtiān qù ná bào. Hǎo ma?
    A: Hǎo.

C Q: _____

   A: _____

E Q: _____

   A: _____

⇨ Please go to page 160 for the answer key.

Radical Lesson 8: 日 (sun)

I. Circle the radical rì 日 and write the following Hànzì according to the rules of bǐshùn.

1. 日 　【rì】　sun; day

2. 明 　【míng】　bright

3. 早 　【zǎo】　(early) morning; Good morning!

4.  【wǎn】 late

5. 是 【shì】 to be; correct; right; yes

6. 明天 【míngtiān】 tomorrow; the near future

II. Transcribe the following pīnyīn text into Hànzì, then give the English translation.

1. Q: Zǎo!

    A: Zǎo!

C Q: _____

    A: _____

E Q: _____

    A: _____

2. Q: Wǒ zhǎo nǐ gēge, tā zài me?

    A: Zài.

C Q: _____

    A: _____

E Q: _____

    A: _____

⇨ Please go to page 160 for the answer key.

Radical Lesson 9: 木 (wood)

I.   Circle the radical mù 木 and write the following Hànzì according to the rules of bǐshùn.

1. 木   【mù】 tree; timber; wood

2. 樹   【shù】 tree

3. 林   【lín】 forest, wood

4. 本 【běn】 root or stem of a plant

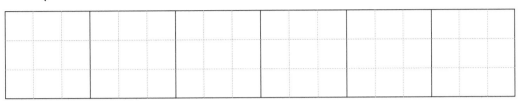

5. 樂 【lè】 be glad to; find pleasure in

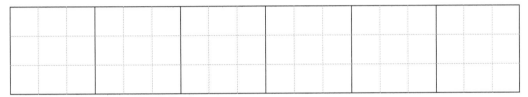

6. 樹木 【shùmù】 trees

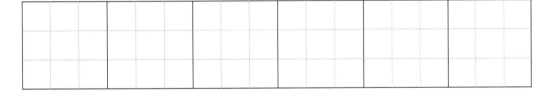

7. 樹林 【shùlín】 woods

8.  【Rìběn】 Japan

9.  【kuàilè】 happy, joyful, cheerful

II. Transcribe the following pīnyīn text into Hànzì, then give the English translation.

1. Tā jiějie míngtiān qù Rìběn.

C _____

_____

E _____

_____

2. Q: Tāa hěn kuàilè. Nǐ ne?

    A: Wǒ yě hěn kuàilè.

C Q: _____

     A: _____

E Q: _____

     A: _____

3. Zhè shùlín hěn dà.

C _____

     _____

E _____

     _____

⇨ Please go to page 161 for the answer key.

⇨ Go to Quiz 6 (Radical Lessons 7–9) on pages 143–45.

Radical Lesson 10: 水 / 氵 (water)

I. Circle the radical shuǐ 水/氵 and write the following Hànzì according to the rules of bǐshùn.

1. 水 【shuǐ】 water; liquid

2. 汽 【qì】 vapor; steam

3. 海 【hǎi】 sea

4.  【tāng】 soup; a surname

5. 酒 【jiǔ】 wine; liquor

6. 冷水 【lěng shuǐ】 cold water

7. 汽水 【qìshuǐ】 soft drink

8.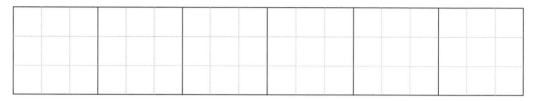

【hǎikǒu】 seaport

9.

【hē tāng】 eat soup

10.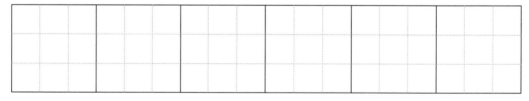

【hē jiǔ】 drink wine or liquor

II. Transcribe the following pīnyīn text into Hànzì, then give the English translation.

1. Q: Nǐ yào hē qìshuǐ, yào hē jiǔ?

   A: Wǒ hē qìshuǐ.

C Q: _____

   A: _____

E Q: _____

   A: _____

2. Wǒ gēge ài hē lěng shuǐ.

C _____

_____

E _____

_____

3. Qǐng hē tāng!

C _____

_____

E _____

_____

➡ Please go to page 161 for the answer key.

Radical Lesson 11: 火 / 灬 (fire)

I. Circle the radical huǒ 火 / 灬 and write the following Hànzì according to the rules of bǐshùn.

1. 火 【huǒ】 fire

2. 災 【zāi】 calamity, disaster

3. 煩 【fán】 be vexed, be irritated, be annoyed; be tired of

4.  燙　【tàng】 very hot, boiling hot

5. 熱　【rè】 heat; hot

6. 火災　【huǒzāi】 fire (as a disaster)

7. 熱心　【rèxīn】 enthusiastic

II. Transcribe the following pīnyīn text into Hànzì, then give the English translation.

1. Zhèr yǒu huǒzāi yě yǒu shuǐzāi.

C _____

   _____

E _____

   _____

2. Wǒ jīntiān hěn fán.

C _____

   _____

E _____

   _____

3. Jīntiān tài rè.

C _____

   _____

E _____

   _____

4. Zhè tāng tài tàng.

C _____

_____

E _____

_____

➡ Please go to page 161
for the answer key.

Radical Lesson 12: 竹 / ⺮ (bamboo)

I. Circle the radical zhú 竹 / ⺮ and write the following Hànzì according to the rules of bǐshùn.

1. 竹 【zhú】 bamboo

2. 筆 【bǐ】 pen

3. 第 【dì】 (ordinal number indicator)

4. 　【děng】　wait; rank; equal

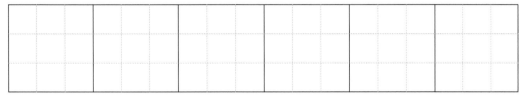

5. 　【bèn】　stupid, foolish, clumsy; dull

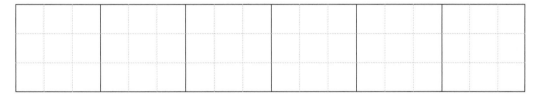

6. 　【dì-yī】　first; foremost

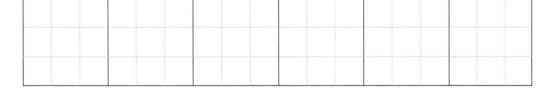

II. Transcribe the following pīnyīn text into Hànzì, then give the English translation.

1. Qǐng nǐ zài zhèr děng wǒ.

C _____

_____

E _____

_____

2. Nǐ yào bǐ ma?

C _____

_____

E _____

_____

3. Jīntiān shì wǒ dì-yī tiān zài Rìběn.

C _____

_____

E _____

_____

4. Tā xiǎng wǒ hěn bèn.

C _____

    _____

E _____

    _____

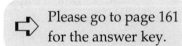
⇨ Please go to page 161
  for the answer key.

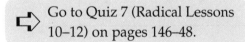
⇨ Go to Quiz 7 (Radical Lessons
  10–12) on pages 146–48.

Radical Lesson 13: 糸 / 纟 (silk)

I. Circle the radical mì 糸 / 纟 and write the following Hànzì according to the rules of bǐshùn.

1. 紙 【zhǐ paper

2. 紅 【hóng】 red

3. 累 【lèi】 tired, fatigued, weary

4. 【jǐn】 tight; urgent; short of money

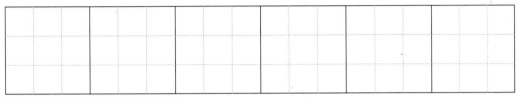

5. 給 【gěi】 give

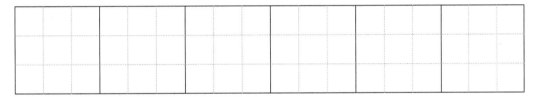

6. 要緊 【yàojǐn】 important, essential

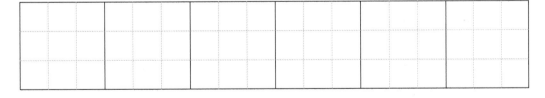

II. Transcribe the following pīnyīn text into Hànzì, then give the English translation.

1. Tā ài hē hóngjiǔ.

C _____

_____

E _____

_____

2. Jiějie yǒu bǐ, mèimei yǒu zhǐ.

C _____

_____

E _____

_____

3. Wǒ jīntiān hěn lèi.

C _____

_____

E _____

_____

4. Qǐng nǐ gěi tā shuǐ hē.

C

_____

_____

E

_____

_____

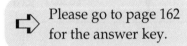 Please go to page 162 for the answer key.

Radical Lesson 14: 艸 / 艹 (grass)

I. Circle the radical cǎo 艸 / 艹 and write the following Hànzì according to the rules of bǐshùn.

1.

   【cǎo】 grass; straw

2.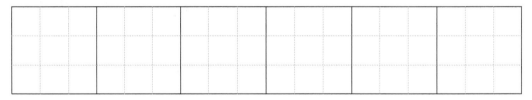

   【chá】 tea

3.

   【yè】 leaf; foliage

4. 菜

【cài】 vegetable; greens; food; dish

5. 花

【huā】 flower; spend

6. 草地

【cǎodì】 grassland, lawn

7. 花茶

【huāchá】 flower tea

8. 茶葉
【cháyè】 tea leaves

9. 酒菜
【jiǔcài】 food and drink; dishes

10. 花生
【huāshēng】 peanut

11. 花草
【huācǎo】 flowers and grasses; plants

II. Transcribe the following pīnyīn text into Hànzì, then give the English translation.

1. Q: Nǐ hē huāchá, tā ne?

    A: Tā hē hóngchá.

C   Q: _____

      A: _____

E   Q: _____

      A: _____

2. Jīntiān jiǔcài dōu hěn hǎo.

C _____

_____

E _____

_____

3. Māma hěn ài huācǎo.

C _____

_____

E _____

_____

➡ Please go to page 162 for the answer key.

Radical Lesson 15: 言 (speech)

I.   Circle the radical yán 言 and write the following Hànzì according to the rules of bǐshùn.

1.   許   【xǔ】 allow, permit; the surname

2.   誰   【shéi】 who; someone

3.   説   【shuō】 speak; talk; say

4.  【huà】 word

5. 【qǐng】 request; ask; invite; please

6. 也 許 【yěxǔ】 perhaps; probably, maybe

7. 小 説 【xiǎoshuō】 novel, fiction

8.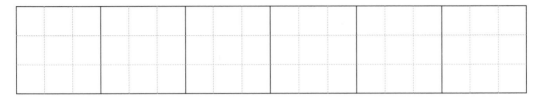

説話 【shuōhuà】 to speak

9.

大話 【dàhuà】 cheat; lie; boast

10.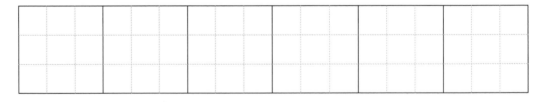

請問 【qǐngwèn】 excuse me, may I ask

II. Transcribe the following pīnyīn text into Hànzì, then give the English translation.

1. Qǐng nǐ shuōhuà!

C _____

_____

E _____

_____

2. Māma xǔ nǐ hē jiǔ ma?

C _____

_____

E _____

_____

3. Shéi ài shuō dàhuà?

C _____

_____

E _____

_____

4.   Nǐ mèimei yǒu xiǎoshuō ma?

C _____

_____

E _____

_____

⇨ Please go to page 162 for the answer key.

⇨ Go to Quiz 8 (Radical Lessons 13–15) on pages 149–52.

Radical Lesson 16: 足 / ⻊ (foot)

I. Circle the radical **zú** 足 / ⻊ and write the following Hànzì according to the rules of bǐshùn.

1. 足

   【**zú**】 foot; sufficient, enough

2. 跑

   【**pǎo**】 run; run away; escape

3. 跳

   【**tiào**】 jump, leap; beat

4. 　【lù】 road, path, way

5. 跟　【gēn】 follow, with, and

6. 手足　【shǒuzú】 brothers and sisters

7. 慢跑　【mànpǎo】 jog

8.

心跳

【xīntiào】 heartbeat, palpitation

9.

路口

【lùkǒu】 crossing, intersection, junction

II. Transcribe the following pīnyīn text into Hànzì, then give the English translation.

1. Qǐng nǐ zài lùkǒu děng tā.

C _____

_____

E _____

_____

2. Tā xīntiào tài kuài. Tā hěn pà.

C _____

_____

E _____

_____

3. Qǐng gēn tā qù Rìběn!

C _____

_____

E _____

_____

4. Tāmen shǒuzú hěn hǎo.

C _____

_____

E _____

_____

➡ Please go to page 162 for the answer key.

Radical Lesson 17: 辵 / 辶 (go, run)

I. Circle the radical zǒuzhī 辵 / 辶 and write the following Hànzì according to the rules of bǐshùn.

1. 近 【jìn】 near, close; closely related

2. 遠 【yuǎn】 far, distant

3. 送 【sòng】 deliver; give as a present; escort, accompany; see somebody off

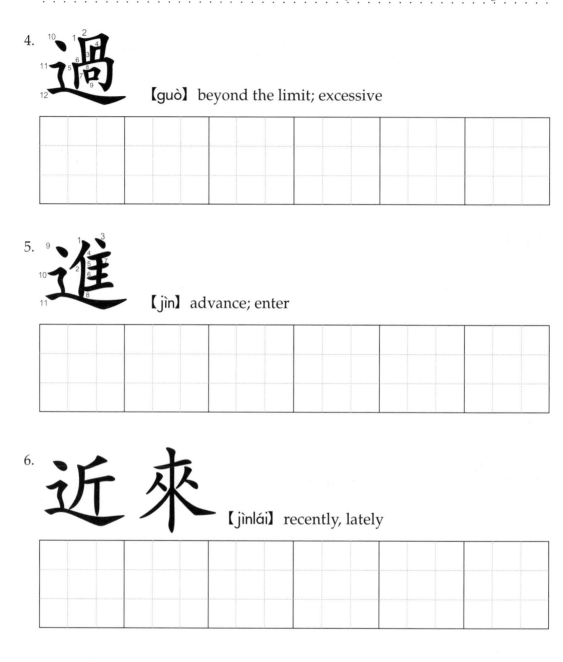

4. 過 【guò】 beyond the limit; excessive

5. 進 【jìn】 advance; enter

6. 近來 【jìnlái】 recently, lately

7. 遠足 【yuǎnzú】 hiking

8. 過來 【guòlai】 come over, come up

9. 進來 【jìnlai】 come (or get) in

10. 進去 【jìnqu】 go in

II. Transcribe the following pīnyīn text into **Hànzì**, then give the English translation.

1. Jìnlái māma hěn lèi.

C _____

_____

E _____

_____

2. Tāmen míngtiān qù yuǎnzú. Nǐ yào qù ma?

C _____

_____

E _____

_____

3. Shéi sòng nǐ huā?

C _____

_____

E _____

_____

4. Shéi sòng nǐ qù Rìběn?

C _____

_____

E _____

_____

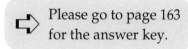
Please go to page 163
for the answer key.

Radical Lesson 18: 金 / 釒 (gold)

I. Circle the radical jīn 金 / 釒 and write the following Hànzì according to the rules of bǐshùn.

1. 金　【jīn】 metals; gold; golden

2. 錢　【qián】 money

3. 銀　【yín】 silver; relating to currency or money

4.

錶

【biǎo】 watch

5.

鉛

【qiān】 lead (metal); lead (in a pencil)

6.

花錢

【huā qián】 spend money

7.

找錢

【zhǎo qián】 give the change

8.

銀行 【yínháng】 bank

9.

金錶 【jīnbiǎo】 gold watch

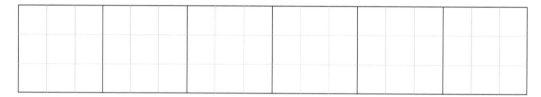

10.

手錶 【shǒubiǎo】 wristwatch

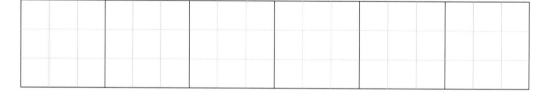

11.

鉛筆 【qiānbǐ】 pencil

II. Transcribe the following pīnyīn text into Hànzì, then give the English translation.

1. Zhè shì jīn shǒubiǎo.

C _____

_____

E _____

_____

2. Tā hěn ài huā qián ma?

C _____

_____

E _____

_____

3. Tāmen dōu yào qiānbǐ. Nǐ ne?

C _____

_____

E _____

_____

4.   Qǐng nǐ zhǎo gěi wǒ qián.

C _____

_____

E _____

_____

⇨ Please go to page 163 for the answer key.

⇨ Go to Quiz 9 (Radical Lessons 16–18) on pages 153–55.

PART 3

· · · · · · · · · · · · · · · · ·

Quizzes on Strokes and Stroke Order / Radicals

Quiz 1
(Strokes and Stroke Order Lessons 1–3)

I.   Write down the pīnyīn with tone markers for the following bǐhuà.

1.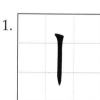

2.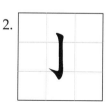

3.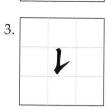

4.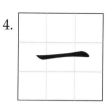

5.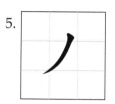

6.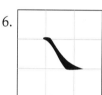

II. Number the bǐshùn and write down the pīnyīn with tone markers for the following Hànzì.

e.g.    sān

1.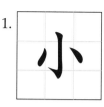

2.

3.

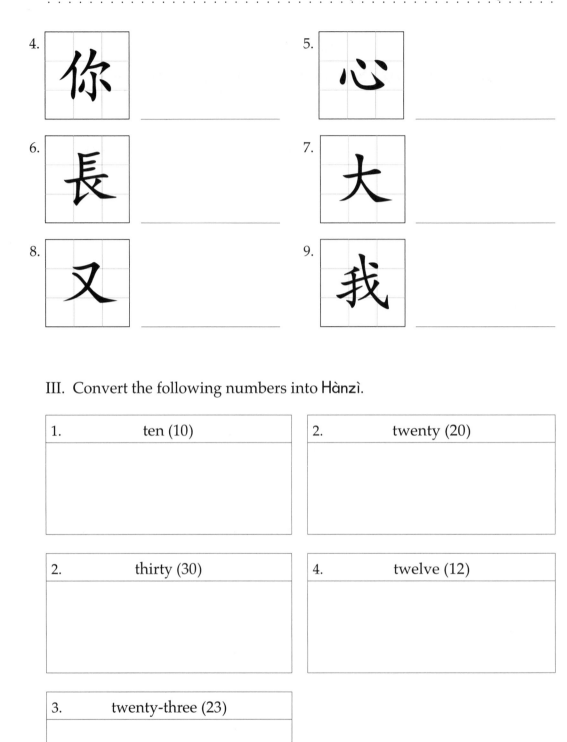

4. 你

5. 心

6. 長

7. 大

8. 又

9. 我

III. Convert the following numbers into Hànzì.

1.   ten (10)

2.   twenty (20)

2.   thirty (30)

4.   twelve (12)

3.   twenty-three (23)

IV. Transcribe the following pīnyīn into Hànzì, then give the English translation.

1. bā tiān

C _____

E _____

2. dàrén

C _____

E _____

3. xiǎoxīn

C _____

E _____

⇨ Please go to page 164 for the answer key.

Quiz 2
(Strokes and Stroke Order Lessons 4–5)

I.   Write down the pīnyīn with tone markers for the following bǐhuà.

1.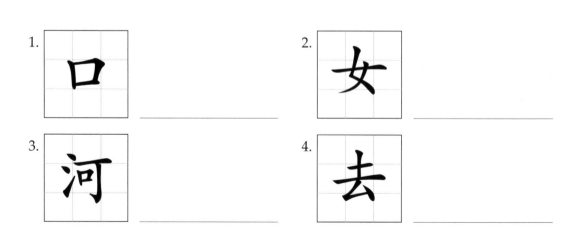

2.

3.

4.

5.

6.

II.   Number the bǐshùn and write down the pīnyīn with tone markers for the following Hànzì.

1. 口

2. 女

3. 河

4. 去

5. 打 _____

6. 班 _____

7. 忙 _____

8. 要 _____

III. Convert the following numbers into Hànzì.

311-221-1233

IV. Transcribe the following pīnyīn into Hànzì, then give the English translation.

1. dàhé

C _____

E _____

2. Wǒ yào tiāntiān qù.

C _____

E _____

3. Nǐ máng.

C _____

E _____

⇨ Please go to pages 164–65 for the answer key.

Quiz 3
(Strokes and Stroke Order Lessons 6–7)

I. Write down the pīnyīn with tone markers for the following bǐhuà.

1. ╰ _____

2. 乙 _____

3. 彡 _____

4. 亅 _____

5. 孑 _____

II. Number the bǐshùn and write down the pīnyīn with tone markers for the following Hànzì.

1. 九 _____

2. 有 _____

3. 吃 _____

4. 這 _____

5.

6.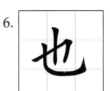

7.

8.

III. Add a stroke to each of the given Hànzì to form another Hànzì.

e.g.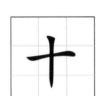

1.

2.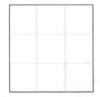

3.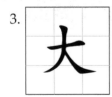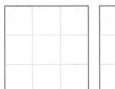

IV. Transcribe the following pīnyīn into Hànzì, then give the English translation.

1. Nǐ wǒ dōu xiǎoxīn.

C _____

E _____

2. Nǐ yào chī ma?

C _____

E _____

3. bāshísān tiān

C _____

E _____

 Please go to page 165 for the answer key.

Quiz 4
(Radical Lessons 1–3)

I. Circle the radical of the following Hànzì. Then write down the name of the radical in pīnyīn with tone markers.

1.

2.

3.

4.

5.

Radical: _____

II. Circle the radical kǒu 口 of the following Hànzì. Write down the total number of strokes for each of them.

1. 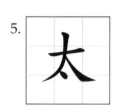 _____

2.  _____

3. 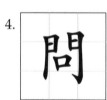 _____

4. _____

5.   _____

III. Write down the pīnyīn with tone markers and the meanings of the following Hànzì.

1. 報 P _____ E _____

2. 坐 P _____ E _____

3. 喝 P _____ E _____

4. 來 P _____ E _____

5. 都 P _____ E _____

IV. Translate the following into Hànzì.

1. Are they coming today?

C _____

2. Mrs. Wang wants to go. Her brother also wants to go.

C _____

_____

3. You sit here with me.

C _____

➡ Please go to pages 165–66 for the answer key.

Quiz 5
(Radical Lessons 4–6)

I. Write down the following basic strokes.

1. piě
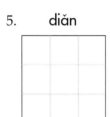

2. héng
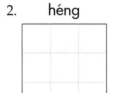

3. shù
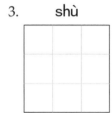

4. nà
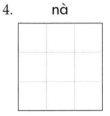

5. diǎn
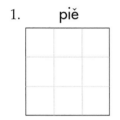

II. Write four Hànzì with each of the following radicals.

1.
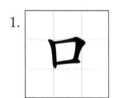 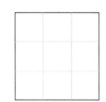 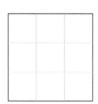

2.
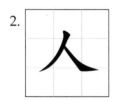 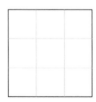 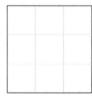 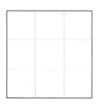

3. 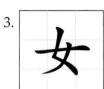

4. 心

III. Circle the radical of the following **Hànzì**. Write down the total number of strokes for each of them.

1. 慢 _____

2. 愛 _____

3. 姓 _____

4. 報 _____

5. 哥 _____

IV. Write down the pīnyīn with tone markers and the meanings of the
following Hànzì.

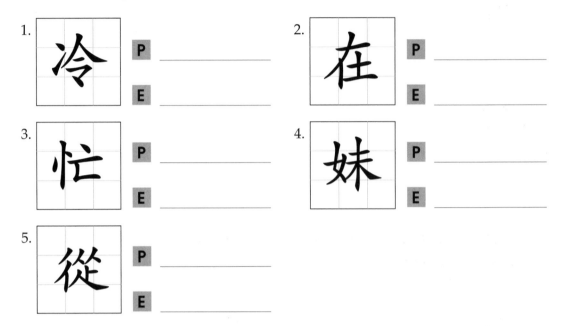

1. 冷 P _____ E _____

2. 在 P _____ E _____

3. 忙 P _____ E _____

4. 妹 P _____ E _____

5. 從 P _____ E _____

V. Translate the following into Hànzì.

1. We miss our mother very much.

C _____

2. I love my little sister and she loves me too.

C _____

⇨ Please go to page 166
for the answer key.

Quiz 6
(Radical Lessons 7–9)
• • • • • • • • • • • • • • • • • • •

I.　Write down the four basic gōu (hooks).

1.　standing
　　hook

2.　flat
　　hook

3.　sleeping
　　hook

4.　slanted
　　hook

II.　Write four Hànzì with each of the following radicals.

1.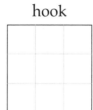

2.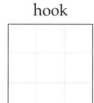

3.

III. Circle the radical of the following Hànzì. Write down the total number
of strokes for each of them.

1.  _____

2.  _____

3. 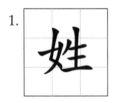 _____

4.  _____

5. _____

IV. Write down the pīnyīn with tone markers and the meanings of the
following Hànzì.

1. P _____
   E _____

2. P _____
   E _____

3. P _____
   E _____

4.  P _____
   E _____

5.  P _____
   E _____

V. Match the following Hànzì with their meanings.

1. 日本 _____

2. 快樂 _____

3. 樹林 _____

4. 姐姐 _____

5. 妹妹 _____

6. 媽媽 _____

7. 今天 _____

8. 明天 _____

9. 快 _____

10. 慢 _____

A. little sister	B. mother	C. slow
D. tomorrow	E. Japan	F. today
G. woods	H. fast	I. happy
J. elder sister		

➡ Please go to page 167 for the answer key.

Quiz 7
(Radical Lessons 10–12)

I. Write down the basic curved hooks.

    1. shù wān gōu   2. héng shù gōu   3. héng zhé gōu

II. Write four Hànzì with each of the following radicals.

1.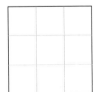

2.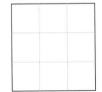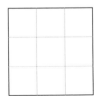

3.

4.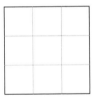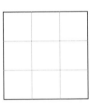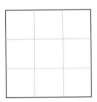

III. Circle the radical of the following Hànzì. Write down the total number
of strokes for each of them.

1. 呢 _____

2. 很 _____

3. 煩 _____

4. 樂 _____

5. 第 _____

IV. Write down the pīnyīn with tone markers and the meanings of the
following Hànzì.

1. 海 P _____
   E _____

2. 燙 P _____
   E _____

3. 熱 P _____
   E _____

4. 笨 P _____
   E _____

5. 竹 P _____
   E _____

V. Match the following Hànzì with their meanings.

1. 第一 _____

2. 火 _____

3. 汽水 _____

4. 喝酒 _____

5. 女人 _____

6. 天天 _____

7. 三十 _____

8. 大河 _____

9. 忙 _____

10. 有 _____

A. have	B. 30	C. busy
D. every day	E. women	F. fire
G. first	H. drink wine	I. big river
J. soft drink		

⇨ Please go to pages 167–68 for the answer key.

Quiz 8
(Radical Lessons 13–15)

I. Write down the pīnyīn with tone markers for the following bǐhuà.

1. 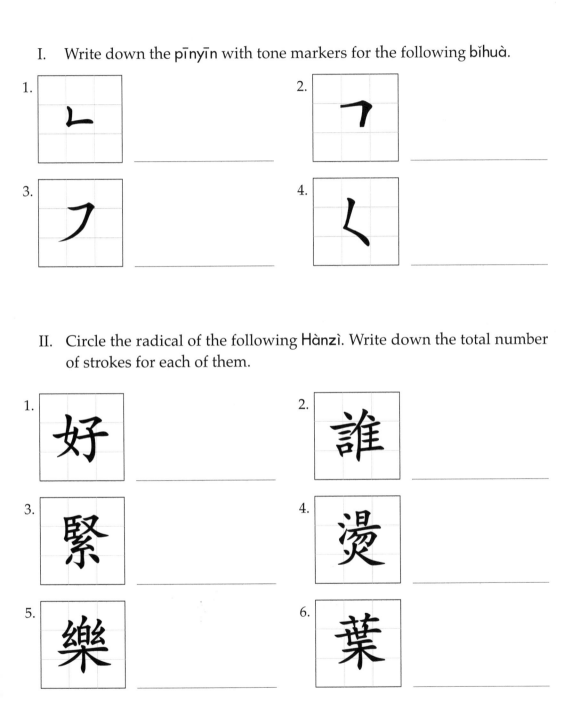 ㄴ _____

2. ㄱ _____

3. ㄱ _____

4. ㄑ _____

II. Circle the radical of the following Hànzì. Write down the total number of strokes for each of them.

1. 好 _____

2. 誰 _____

3. 緊 _____

4. 燙 _____

5. 樂 _____

6. 葉 _____

7. _____

8. _____

9. _____

10. _____

III. Write down the pīnyīn with tone markers and the meanings of the following Hànzì.

1.  **P** _____

   E _____

2. **P** _____

   E _____

3. **P** _____

   E _____

4. **P** _____

   E _____

5.  **P** _____

   E _____

V. Form double-syllable words with the following Hànzì. Write down the meanings of the words formed.

e.g.

説 話　　E _____ to talk / speak _____

1. 哥　　　E _____

2. 妹　　　E _____

3. 　樂　　E _____

4. 　地　　E _____

5. 日　　　E _____

6. 天　　E _____

7. 明　　E _____

8. 生　　E _____

9. 足　　E _____

➡ Please go to pages 168–69 for the answer key.

Quiz 9
(Radical Lessons 16–18)

I.   Write down the following strokes.

1.   héng zhé
     piě

2.   héng zhé
     wān gōu

3.   tí

4.   shù gōu

II.   Circle the radical of the following Hànzì.

1.

2.

3.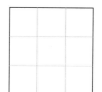

4.

5.

6.

7.

8.

9.

III. Write down the pīnyīn with tone markers and the meanings of the
following Hànzì.

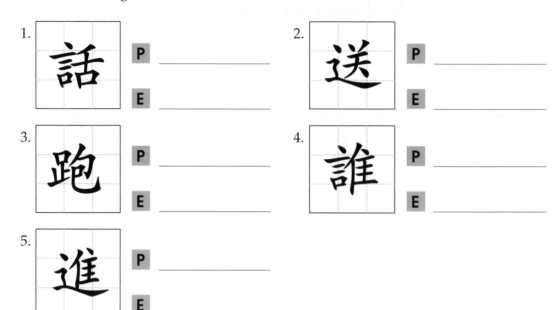

1. 話   P _____
         E _____

2. 送   P _____
         E _____

3. 跑   P _____
         E _____

4. 誰   P _____
         E _____

5. 進   P _____
         E _____

IV. Match the following Hànzì with their meanings.

1. 近來 _____   2. 進來 _____

3. 要緊 _____   4. 土地 _____

5. 熱心 _____   6. 也許 _____

7. 慢跑 _____   8. 鉛筆 _____

9. 找錢 _____   10. 銀行 _____

A. enthusiastic	B. important	C. maybe
D. jog	E. recently	F. come in
G. pencil	H. bank	I. give change
J. earth		

V. Translate the following pīnyīn into Hànzì, then give the English translation.

1. Qǐngwèn tā shì shéi?

C _____

E _____

2. Nǐ yǒu jīnbiǎo ma?

C _____

E _____

3. Jīntiān wǒ yào hé mèimei qù mànpǎo.

C _____

E _____

⇨ Please go to page 169 for the answer key.

PART *4*

· · · · · · · · · · · · · · · · ·

Answer Keys
for
Radical Lessons / Quizzes

Answer Keys for Radical Lessons

Radical Lesson 1

1. **C** Q: 他們今天來嗎？

   A: 來。

   E Q: Are they coming today?

   A: Yes (they are coming).

2. **C** Q: 王太太今天來嗎？

   A: 她也來。

   E Q: Is Mrs. Wang coming today?

   A: She is coming too.

Radical Lesson 2

1. **C** 他要去問哥哥，你呢？

   E He is going to ask his elder brother. How about you?

2. **C** 他和我都要去問哥哥。

   E (Both) he and I are going to ask (our) elder brother.

3. **C** 你要喝。我也要喝。

   E You want to drink. I want to drink too.

Radical Lesson 3

1. **C** 他們有土地嗎？

   E Do they have (their) land?

2. **C** 我們坐在這兒。

   E We sit here.

3. **C** Q: 報在這兒嗎？

   A: 在。

   E Q: Is the newspaper here?

   A: Yes.

Radical Lesson 4

1. **C** Q: 你姐姐，妹妹好嗎？

   A: 她們都好。

   E Q: How are your elder sister and your little sister?

   A: They are fine.

2. **C** 你姓王。我也姓王。

   E Your family name is Wang. Mine is Wang too.

Radical Lesson 5

1. **C** 我後天得去。

   E I must go the day after tomorrow.

2. **C** 王太太待我很好。

   E Mrs. Wang treats me very well.

3. **C** 我明天得從這兒去。

   E I must leave from here tomorrow.

Radical Lesson 6

1. **C** 他們很想媽媽。

   E They miss their mother very much.

2. **C** 你妹妹怕哥哥嗎？

   E Is your little sister afraid of your elder brother?

3. **C** 你太快，我太慢。

   E You are too fast; I am too slow.

4. **C** Q: 你愛我嗎？

   A: 愛。

   E Q: Do you love me?

   A: Yes.

Radical Lesson 7

1. **C** 王太太找你。

   E Mrs. Wang has been looking for you.

2. **C** 他手指很長。

   E His fingers are very long.

3. **C** Q: 我明天去拿報，好嗎？

   A: 好。

   E Q: I will get the newspaper tomorrow, okay?

   A: Okay.

Radical Lesson 8

1. **C** Q: 早！

   A: 早！

   E Q: Good morning!

   A: Good morning.

2. **C** Q: 我找你哥哥，他在嗎？

   A: 在。

   E Q: I'm looking for your elder brother. Is he home?

   A: Yes.

Radical Lesson 9

1. **C** 他姐姐明天去<u>日本</u>。
   E His elder sister is going to Japan tomorrow.
2. **C** Q: 他很快樂。你呢？
      A: 我也很快樂。
   E Q: He's very happy. How about you?
      A: I'm very happy too.
3. **C** 這樹林很大。
   E This wood is vast.

Radical Lesson 10

1. **C** Q: 你要喝汽水，要喝酒？
      A: 我喝汽水。
   E Q: Which do you like to have? Soft drink or wine?
      A: I'd like to have soft drink.
2. **C** 我哥哥愛喝冷水。
   E My elder brother likes drinking cold water.
3. **C** 請喝湯！
   E Please have some soup!

Radical Lesson 11

1. **C** 這兒有火災也有水災。
   E There have been fire and flooding cases.
2. **C** 我今天很煩。
   E I feel very annoyed today.
3. **C** 今天太熱。
   E It is too hot today.
4. **C** 這湯太燙。
   E This soup is too hot.

Radical Lesson 12

1. **C** 請你在這兒等我。
   E Please wait for me here.
2. **C** 你要筆嗎？
   E Do you need a pen?
3. **C** 今天是我第一天在<u>日本</u>。
   E Today is my first day in Japan.
4. **C** 他想我很笨。
   E He thinks that I am stupid.

Radical Lesson 13

1. **C** 他愛喝紅酒。

   E He likes drinking red wine.

2. **C** 姐姐有筆，妹妹有紙。

   E The elder sister has a pencil; the little sister has a paper.

3. **C** 我今天很累。

   E I am very tired today.

4. **C** 請你給他水喝。

   E Please give him some water to drink.

Radical Lesson 14

1. **C** Q: 你喝花茶，他呢？

   A: 他喝紅茶。

   E Q: You would like to have flower tea. What about him?

   A: He would like to have red (black) tea.

2. **C** 今天酒菜都很好。

   E All the dishes today are good.

3. **C** 媽媽很愛花草。

   E Mother likes plants very much.

Radical Lesson 15

1. **C** 請你說話！

   E Please say something!

2. **C** 媽媽許你喝酒嗎？

   E Has your mother allowed you to drink?

3. **C** 誰愛說大話？

   E Who likes to cheat?

4. **C** 你妹妹有小說嗎？

   E Has you little sister got any novel?

Radical Lesson 16

1. **C** 請你在路口等他。

   E Please wait for him at the junction.

2. **C** 他心跳太快。他很怕。

   E His heart is beating too fast. He is very frightened.

3. **C** 請跟他去<u>日本</u>！

   E Please go to Japan with him!

4. **C** 他們手足很好。

   E They (brothers) get along very well.

Radical Lesson 17

1. **C** 近來媽媽很累。
   E Mother has been very tired recently.

2. **C** 他們明天去遠足。你要去嗎？
   E They are going on a hiking trip tomorrow. Do you want to join in?

3. **C** 誰送你花？
   E Who gave you the flowers?

4. **C** 誰送你去<u>日本</u>？
   E Who sent / is sending you off to Japan?

Radical Lesson 18

1. **C** 這是金手錶。
   E This is a gold watch.

2. **C** 他很愛花錢嗎？
   E Does he like spending money?

3. **C** 他們都要鉛筆。你呢？
   E They all want pencils. How about you?

4. **C** 請你找給我錢。
   E Please give me the change.

Answer Keys for Quizzes

Quiz 1 (Stroke and Stroke Order Lessons 1–3)

I. 1. shù   2. shù gōu   3. shù gōu
    4. héng   5. piě   6. nà

II. 1.   2.   3.   4.   5.
       xiǎo   tiān   shí   nǐ   xīn

    6.   7.   8.   9.
       cháng   dà   yòu   wǒ

III. 1. 十   2. 二十   3. 三十   4. 十二   5. 二十三

IV. 1. **C** 八天
       E eight days
    2. **C** 大人
       E adults
    3. **C** 小心
       E be careful

Quiz 2 (Stroke and Stroke Order Lessons 4–5)

I. 1. xié zhé   2. diǎn   3. wò gōu
    4. tí   5. héng zhé   6. héng gōu

II. 1. 口   2. 女   3. 河   4. 去
       kǒu   nǚ   hé   qù

    5. 打   6. 班   7. 忙   8. 要
       dǎ   bān   máng   yào

III. 三一一　　二二一　　一二三三

IV. 1. **C** 大河

    E big river

  2. **C** 我要天天去。

    E I would like to go every day.

  3. **C** 你忙。

    E You are busy.

Quiz 3 (Stroke and Stroke Order Lessons 6–7)

I. 1. shù zhé gōu   2. héng zhé gōu   3. héng zhé piě

  4. héng shù gōu   5. héng piě wān gōu

II. 1.  jiǔ   2. yǒu   3. chī   4. zhè

  5. nà/nèi   6. yě   7. jiàn   8. yuàn

III. 1. 三   2. 大   3. 太 / 天

IV. 1. **C** 你我都小心。

    E (Both)You and I are careful.

  2. **C** 你要吃嗎？

    E Do you want to eat?

  3. **C** 八十三天

    E eight-three days

Quiz 4 (Radical Lessons 1–3)

I. 1.   2.    3.   4.   5.

Radical: 人 / 亻 (rén)

II. 1. 嗎　2. 哥　3. 和　4. 問　5. 吃

13　　　　10　　　　8　　　　10　　　　6

III. 1. **P** bào
     E newspaper
2. **P** zuò
     E sit

3. **P** hē
     E to drink
4. **P** lái
     E come

5. **P** dōu
     E all

IV. 1. **C** 他們今天來嗎？

2. **C** 王太太要去，她哥哥也要去。

3. **C** 你和我坐在這兒。

Quiz 5 (Radical Lessons 4–6)

I. 1. ノ　2. 一　3. 丨　4. 丶　5. 八

II. 1. 和　問　哥　呢

2. 們　今　太　他

3. 姓　妹　姐　好

4. 快　怕　愛　想

III. 1. 慢　2. 愛　3. 姓　4. 報　5. 哥

14　　　　13　　　　8　　　　12　　　　10

IV. 1. **P** lěng
     E cold
2. **P** zài
     E at / in / on

3. **P** máng
     E busy
4. **P** mèi
     E little sister

5. **P** cóng
     E from

V. 1. **C** 我們很想我們媽媽。

2. **C** 我愛我妹妹，她也愛我。

Quiz 6 (Radical Lessons 7–9)

I.   1.   2.   3.   4.

II.   1. 指 找 才 拿

     2. 明 晚 是 早

     3. 林 本 樹 樂

III. 1. 好   2. 後   3. 怕   4. 拿   5. 是

         6   9   8   10   9

IV. 1. **P** xìng   2. **P** cái
      E surname   **E** just

    3. **P** zhǎo   4. **P** wǎn
      E looking for   **E** late

    5. **P** mù
      E timber / wood / tree

V.   1. E   2. I   3. G   4. J   5. A
     6. B   7. F   8. D   9. H   10. C

Quiz 7 (Radical Lessons 10–12)

I.   1.   2.   3.

II.   1. 酒 海 湯 汽

     2. 笨 等 筆 第

     3. 燙 煩 災 熱

     4. 在 地 坐 報

III. 1. 呢   2. 很   3. 煩   4. 樂   5. 第

         8   9   13   15   11

IV. 1. **P** hǎi   2. **P** tàng
     E sea   **E** boiling hot

     3. **P** rè   4. **P** bèn
     E hot / heat   **E** stupid / dull

     5. **P** zhú
     E bamboo

V. 1. G   2. F   3. J   4. H   5. E
    6. D   7. B   8. I   9. C   10. A

Quiz 8 (Radical Lessons 13–15)

I. 1. shù zhé   2. héng zhé   3. héng piě   4. xié zhé

II. 1.   2.   3.   4.   5.
       6   15   15   16   15

    6.   7.   8.   9.   10.
       12   6   7   12   9

III. 1. **P** huà   2. **P** xǔ
     E word   **E** allow / permit

     3. **P** tāng   4. **P** bǐ
     E soup   **E** pen

     5. **P** gěi
     E to give

IV. 1. **C** 哥
     E elder brother

     2. **C** 妹
     E younger sister

     3. **C** 快
     E happy

     4. **C** 土
     E earth / land / ground

     5. **C** 本
     E Japan

6. **C** 今
   E today

7. **C** 天
   E tomorrow

8. **C** 花
   E peanut

9. **C** 遠
   E hiking

Quiz 9 (Radical Lessons 16–18)

I. 1.   2.   3.   4.

II. 1. 錢   2. 遠   3. 累   4. 請   5. 煙
    6. 指   7. 坐   8. 太   9. 後

III. 1. **P** huà   2. **P** sòng
     E word   **E** deliver

3. **P** pǎo   4. **P** shéi
   E run   **E** who

5. **P** jìn
   E enter / advance

IV. 1. E   2. F   3. B   4. J   5. A
    6. C   7. D   8. G   9. I   10. H

V. 1. **C** 請問，他是誰？
      E Excuse me, who is he?

2. **C** 你有金錶嗎？
   E Have you got a gold watch?

3. **C** 今天我要和妹妹去慢跑。
   E Today I go jogging with my sister.

Appendixes

· · · · · · · · · · · · · · · · ·

Index: Strokes and Stroke Order Lessons

Pīnyīn	Hànzì	English	Page
B			
bā	八	eight	11, 12, 14
bā tiān	八天	eight days	16
bān	班	class	35, 37, 39
bāshí tiān	八十天	eighty days	17
C			
cháng	長	long	20, 21, 23
chī	吃	to eat	43, 45, 47
D			
dà	大	big	11, 12, 14
dà bān	大班	big class	40
dà hé	大河	big river	39
dǎ	打	hit; play	35, 36, 39
dǎ qiú	打球	to play ball	42
dǎ rén	打人	to hit someone	41
dàrén	大人	adult	15
dàxiǎo	大小	big and small; size	25
dōu	都	all	50, 52, 54
E			
èr	二	two	3, 4, 6
èrshí	二十	twenty	8
èrshísān	二十三	twenty-three	9
H			
hé	河	river	35, 36, 38
J			
jiàn	建	to build	50, 51, 53

Pīnyīn	Hànzì	English	Page
jiǔ	九	nine	43, 44, 46
jiǔshíjiǔ	九十九	ninety-nine	48
K			
kǒu	口	mouth	28, 30
L			
lěng	冷	cold	35, 38
lěng tiān	冷天	cold weather	41
M			
ma	嗎	(question marker)	43, 45, 47
máng	忙	busy	28, 30
N			
nà/nèi	那	that	50, 51, 53
Nà hé cháng ma?	那河長嗎	Is that river long?	55
Nà rén yào qù.	那人要去	That person wants to go.	54
nǐ	你	you	20, 21, 23
Nǐ qù!	你去	You go!	33
Nǐ wǒ dōu máng.	你我都忙	Both you and I are busy.	56
Nǐ yě chī ma?	你也吃嗎	Do you eat too?	49
Nǐ yǒu qiú ma?	你有球嗎	Do you have a ball?	49
Nǐ xiǎoxīn!	你小心	You be careful!	26
nǚ	女	female	28, 29, 30
nǚrén	女人	woman, women	32
Q			
qiú	球	ball	35, 36, 38
qù	去	go	28, 29, 31
R			
rén	人	human being; person	11, 12, 14
rénkǒu	人口	population	31
rùkǒu	入口	entrance	32

Pīnyīn	Hànzì	English	Page
S			
sān	三	three	3, 4, 6
sānshí	三十	thirty	9
sānshíyí	三十一	thirty-one	10
shí	十	ten	3, 5, 7
shí tiān	十天	ten days	16
shíbā rén	十八人	eighteen people	18
shíjiǔ	十九	nineteen	47
shísān	十三	thirteen	8
shíyī	十一	eleven	7
T			
tiān	天	sky; day	11, 13, 15
tiāntiān	天天	every day, daily	17
W			
wáng	王	king; a surname	3, 5, 7
wǒ	我	I, me	20, 22, 24
Wǒ chī.	我吃	I eat.	48
Wǒ máng.	我忙	I am busy.	33
Wǒ xiǎoxīn.	我小心	I am careful.	26
Wǒ yào qù.	我要去	I want to go.	34
X			
xiǎo	小	small	20, 21, 23
xiǎo bān	小班	small class	40
xiǎorén	小人	villain; vile character	25
Xiǎoxīn!	小心	Be careful; take care!	24
xīn	心	heart; mind	20, 22, 24
Y			
yào	要	want	28, 29, 31
yě	也	also	43, 44, 46
yī	一	one	3, 4, 6
yǒu	有	have	43, 44, 46

Pīnyīn	Hànzì	English	Page
yòu	又	again	11, 13, 15
yuàn	院	courtyard, yard	50, 52, 54
Z			
zhè/zhèi	這	this	50, 51, 53
zhè rén hǎo ma?	這人好嗎	Is this person good?	55

Index: Radical Lessons

Pīnyīn	Hànzì	Bùshǒu	English	Page
A				
ài	愛	心 / 忄	love, affection; like, be fond of	76
B				
bào	報	土 / 土	newspaper	67
běn	本	木	root or stem of a plant	85
bèn	笨	竹 / ⺮	stupid, foolish, clumsy; dull	97
bǐ	筆	竹 / ⺮	pen	96
biǎo	錶	金 / 金	watch	123
C				
cái	才	手 / 扌	just	79
cài	菜	艸 / ⺾	vegetable; greens; food; dish	105
cǎo	草	艸 / ⺾	grass; straw	104
cǎodì	草地		grassland, lawn	105
chá	茶	艸 / ⺾	tea	104
cháyè	茶葉		tea leaves	106
cóng	從	彳	from	73
D				
dàhuà	大話		cheat; lie; boast	110
dài	待	彳	treat, deal with	73
děi	得	彳	need; must; have to	72
děng	等	竹 / ⺮	wait; rank; equal	97
dì	地	土 / 土	earth; land; ground	66
dì	第	竹 / ⺮	(ordinal number indicator)	96
dì-yī	第一		first; foremost	97
F				
fán	煩	火 / 灬	be vexed, be irritated, be annoyed; be tired of	92

Pīnyīn	Hànzì	Bùshǒu	English	Page
G				
gěi	給	糸 / 糹	give	101
gēn	跟	足 / 𧾷	follow, with, and	114
gē	哥	口	elder brother	63
gēge	哥哥		elder brother	64
guò	過	辵 / 辶	beyond the limit; excessive	118
guòlai	過來		come over, come up	119
H				
hǎi	海	水 / 氵	sea	88
hǎikǒu	海口		seaport	90
hǎo	好	女	good, fine, nice; kind	70
hē	喝	口	drink	63
hē jiǔ	喝酒		drink wine or liquor	90
hē tāng	喝湯		eat soup	90
hé	和	口	together with, and	64
hěn	很	彳	very; quite; awfully	72
hóng	紅	糸 / 糹	red	100
hòu	後	彳	back, behind, rear	72
hòutiān	後天		the day after tomorrow	73
huā	花	艸 / 艹	flower; spend	105
huā qián	花錢		spend money	123
huācǎo	花草		flowers and grasses; plants	106
huāchá	花茶		flower tea	105
huāshēng	花生		peanut	106
huà	話	言	word	109
huǒ	火	火 / 灬	fire	92
huǒzāi	火災		fire (as a disaster)	93
J				
jiě	姐	女	elder sister	69
jiějie	姐姐		elder sister	70
jīn	今	人 / 亻	modern; present-day	59
jīn	金	金 / 釒	metals; gold; golden	122

Pīnyīn	Hànzì	Bùshǒu	English	Page
jīnbiǎo	金錶		gold watch	124
jīntiān	今天		today	61
jìn	近	辵/辶	near, close; closely related	117
jìn	進	辵/辶	advance; enter	118
jìnlai	進來		come (or get) in	119
jìnlái	近來		recently, lately	118
jìnqu	進去		go in	119
jǐn	緊	系/糸	tight; urgent; short of money	101
jiǔ	酒	水/氵	wine; liquor	89
jiǔcài	酒菜		food and drink; dishes	106

K

| kuài | 快 | 心/忄 | fast, quick; hurry up; soon | 75 |
| kuàilè | 快樂 | | happy, joyful, cheerful | 86 |

L

lái	來	人/亻	come; arrive	60
lè	樂	木	be glad to; find pleasure in	85
lèi	累	系/糸	tired, fatigued, weary	100
lěng shuǐ	冷水		cold water	89
lín	林	木	forest, wood	84
lù	路	足/𧾷	road, path, way	114
lùkǒu	路口		crossing, intersection, junction	115

M

mā	媽	女	mom, mother	69
māma	媽媽		mom, mother	70
màn	慢	心/忄	slow	75
mànpǎo	慢跑		jog	114
mèi	妹	女	younger sister	69
mèimei	妹妹		younger sister	71
men	們	人/亻	person (plural)	59
míng	明	日	bright	81
míngtiān	明天		tomorrow; the near future	82

Pīnyīn	Hànzì	Bùshǒu	English	Page
mù	木	木	tree; timber; wood	84
N				
ná	拿	手 / 扌	hold; take; seize	79
ne	呢	口	(question marker)	64
nǐmen	你們		you (plural)	60
P				
pà	怕	心 / 忄	fear; dread; be afraid of	76
pǎo	跑	足 / 𧾷	run; run away; escape	113
Q				
qì	汽	水 / 氵	vapour; steam	88
qiān	鉛	金 / 釒	lead (metal); lead (in a pencil)	123
qiānbǐ	鉛筆		pencil	124
qián	錢	金 / 釒	money	122
qǐng	請	言	request; ask; invite; please	109
qǐngwèn	請問		excuse me, may I ask	110
qìshuǐ	汽水		soft drink	89
R				
rè	熱	火 / 灬	heat; hot	93
rèxīn	熱心		enthusiastic	93
rì	日	日	sun; day	81
Rìběn	日本		Japan	86
S				
shéi	誰	言	who; someone	108
shì	是	日	to be; correct; right; yes	82
shǒu	手	手 / 扌	hand	78
shǒubiǎo	手錶		wristwatch	124
shǒuxīn	手心		palm	79
shǒuzhǐ	手指		finger	79
shǒuzú	手足		brothers and sisters	114
shù	樹	木	tree	84

Pīnyīn	Hànzì	Bùshǒu	English	Page
shuǐ	水	水/氵	water; liquid	88
shùlín	樹林		woods	85
shùmù	樹木		trees	85
shuō	說	言	speak; talk; say	108
shuōhuà	說話		to speak	110
sòng	送	辵/辶	deliver; give as a present; escort; accompany see somebody off	117
T				
tā	他	人/亻	he; she; him; her	59
tài	太	人/亻	excessively, too; very	60
tàitai	太太		Mrs.; wife	61
tài dà	太大		too big	61
tāmen	他們		they; them (plural)	61
tāng	湯	水/氵	soup; a surname	89
tàng	燙	火/灬	very hot, boiling hot	93
tiào	跳	足/𧾷	jump, leap; beat	113
tǔ	土	土/圡	soil; earth	66
tǔdì	土地		land	67
W				
wǎn	晚	日	late	82
wèn	問	口	ask, inquire	63
wǒmen	我們		we; us	60
X				
xiǎng	想	心/忄	think; suppose; consider; miss; would like to	76
xiǎoshuō	小說		novel, fiction	109
xìng	姓	女	surname, family name	70
xīntiào	心跳		heartbeat, palpitation	115
xǔ	許	言	allow, permit; the surname	108
Y				
yàojǐn	要緊		important, essential	101
yè	葉	艸/艹	leaf; foliage	104

Pīnyīn	Hànzì	Bùshǒu	English	Page
yěxǔ	也許		perhaps; probably, maybe	109
yín	銀	金 / 釒	silver; relating to currency or money	122
yínháng	銀行		bank	124
yuǎn	遠	辵 / 辶	far, distant	117
yuǎnzú	遠足		hiking	118
Z				
zāi	災	火 / 灬	calamity, disaster	92
zài	在		at; in; on; exist	67
zǎo	早	日	(early) morning; Good morning!	81
zhǎo	找	手 / 扌	look for, try to find; call on, ask for	78
zhǎo qián	找錢		give the change	123
zhǐ	紙	糸 / 糹	paper	100
zhǐ	指	手 / 扌	finger; point at; point to	78
zhú	竹	竹 / 竹	bamboo	96
zú	足	足 / 𧾷	foot; sufficient, enough	113
zuò	坐	土 / 圡	sit; take a seat; travel by (plant, train, etc.)	66

Flash Cards for Strokes and Stroke Order Lessons

Lesson 1	Lesson 2	Lesson 3	Lesson 4
一	人	小	口
二	八	長	忙
三	大	你	女
十	天	我	要
王	又	心	去

Lesson 5	Lesson 6	Lesson 7
冷	也	建
河	有	這
球	九	那
打	吃	都
班	嗎	院

Flash Cards for Radical Lessons

Lesson 1	Lesson 2	Lesson 3	Lesson 4
他	喝	土	媽
們	問	地	姐
令	哥	坐	妹
太	和	在	好
來	呢	報	姓

Lesson 5	Lesson 6	Lesson 7	Lesson 8

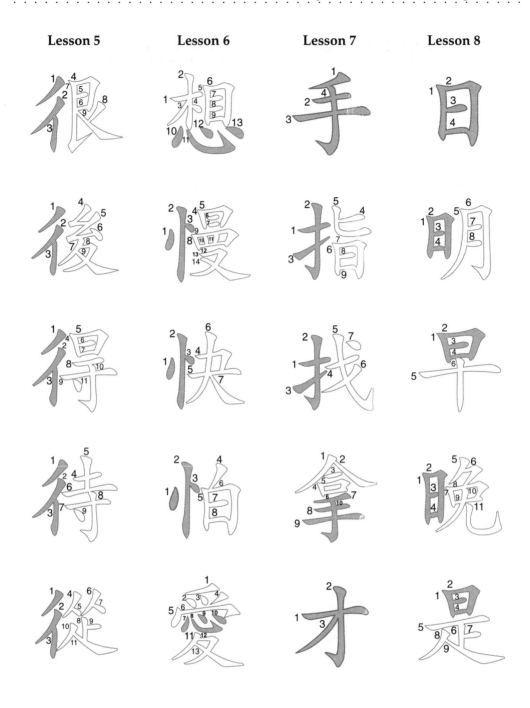

Lesson 9	Lesson 10	Lesson 11	Lesson 12
木	水	火	竹
樹	汽	災	筆
林	海	煩	第
本	湯	熨	等
樂	酒	熱	笨

Lesson 13	Lesson 14	Lesson 15	Lesson 16

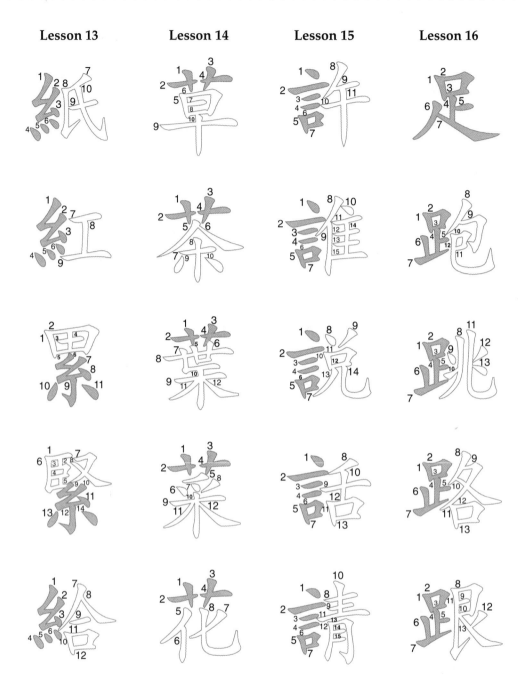

Lesson 17   **Lesson 18**

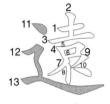

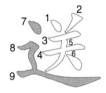 

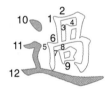 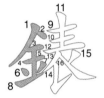

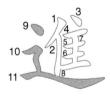

79 Common Chinese Radicals

Radical	Chinese Name	English Meaning	Examples		
一	yì héng 一橫	one	shàng 上	wǔ 五	qī 七
丨	yí shù 一豎	down stroke	zhōng 中	yā 丫	chuàn 串
乙	yǐ zì bù 乙字部	one	yǐ 乙	yě 也	gān 乾
*人/亻	dān rén 單人	single man	nǐ 你	jīn 今	yǐ 以
入	rù zì bù 入字部	enter	rù 入	liǎng 兩	quán 全
八	bā zì bù 八字部	eight	liù 六	gōng 公	diǎn 典
冫	liǎng diǎn bīng 兩點冰	ice	bīng 冰	lěng 冷	dōng 冬
刀/刂	dāo zì bù 刀字部	knife	fēn 分	qiē 切	dào 到
力	lì zì bù 力字部	strength	zhù 助	jiā 加	nǔ 努

* One of the most frequently-used radicals introduced in the text.

十	shí zì bù 十字部	ten	wǔ 午	bǎn 半	nán 南
又	yòu zì bù 又字部	hand; also	yòu 又	yōu 友	qǔ 取
* 口	kǒu zì bù 口字部	mouth	chī 吃	gào 告	ma 嗎
口	dà kǒu 大口	enclosure	sì 四	guó 國	huí 回
* 土	tǔ zì bù 土字部	earth	dì 地	zuò 坐	zài 在
夕	xī zì bù 夕字部	evening	duō 多	wài 外	yè 夜
大	dà zì bù 大字部	big	tài 太	tiān 天	fū 夫
* 女	nǚ zì bù 女字部	woman	xìng 姓	hǎo 好	mā 媽
子	zǐ zì bù 子字部	child	hái 孩	zì 字	xué 學
宀	bǎo gài tóu 包蓋頭	roof	kè 客	jiā 家	ān 安
寸	cùn zì bù 寸字部	inch	duì 對	jiāng 將	dǎo 導
小	xiǎo zì bù 小字部	small	xiǎo 小	shǎo 少	jiān 尖

尸	shī zì bù 尸字部	corpse	chǐ 尺	wū 屋	shī 屍
山	shān zì bù 山字部	mountain	shān 山	yuè 岳	dǎo 島
巾	jīn zì bù 巾字部	handkerchief	shī 師	dài 帶	bāng 幫
干	gān zì bù 干字部	shield	píng 平	xíng 幸	gān 幹
广	guǎng zì bù 广字部	shelter	zuò 座	dǐ 底	guǎng 廣
弓	gōng zì bù 弓字部	bow	zhāng 張	dì 弟	qiáng 強
* 彳	shuāng lì rén 雙立人	double man	hěn 很	hòu 後	wǎng 往
* 心/忄	xīn zì bù 心字部	heart	xiǎng 想	bì 必	pà 怕
戈	gē zì bù 戈字部	spear	chéng 成	wǒ 我	huò 或
* 手/扌	shǒu zì bù 手字部	hand	dǎ 打	zhǎo 找	ná 拿
文	fǎn wén 反文	tap	shōu 收	gù 故	jiào 教
斤	jīn zì bù 斤字部	axe	fǔ 斧	xīn 新	duàn 斷

			zǎo 早	míng 明	shì 是
* 日	rì zì bù 日字部	sun			
曰	yuē zì bù 日字部	say	shū 書	gèng 更	zuì 最
月	yuè zì bù 月字部	moon	péng 朋	wàng 望	yǒu 有
* 木	mù zì bù 木字部	wood	běn 本	lǐ 李	xiào 校
止	zhǐ zì bù 止字部	stop	zhèng 正	cǐ 此	bù 步
* 水/氵	shuǐ zì bù 水字部	water	hé 河	qì 汽	shuǐ 水
* 火/灬	huǒ zì páng/sì diǎn huǒ 火字旁/四點火	fire	dēng 燈	zhào 照	rè 熱
父	fù zì bù 父字部	father	fù 父	bà 爸	yé 爺
牛	niú zì bù 牛字部	ox	wù 物	tè 特	láo 牢
用	yòng zì bù 用字部	use	yòng 用	shuǎi 甩	béng 甭
玉/王	yù zì bù 玉字部	jade	xiàn 現	wán 玩	bān 班

甘	gān zì bù 甘字部	sweet	gān 甘	tián 甜	shèn 甚
田	tián zì bù 田字部	field	nán 男	liú 留	huà 畫
疒	bìng zì bù 病字部	sickness	bìng 病	téng 疼	yǎng 癢
白	bái zì bù 白字部	white	bǎi 百	de 的	huáng 皇
目	mù zì bù 目字部	eye	kàn 看	yǎn 眼	xiāng 相
石	shí zì bù 石字部	stone	wǎn 碗	dié 碟	kuàng 礦
示	shì zì bù 示字部	show	shén 神	lǐ 禮	piào 票
禾	hé zì bù 禾字部	grain	zhǒng 種	qiū 秋	kē 科
穴	xué zì bù 穴字部	hole	kōng 空	chuān 穿	jiū 究
立	lì zì bù 立字部	stand	zhàn 站	zhāng 章	tóng 童
* 竹/ ⺮	zhú zì bù 竹字部	bamboo	bǐ 筆	bèn 笨	dì 第
米	mǐ zì bù 米字部	rice	fěn 粉	jīng 精	cū 粗

部首	名稱	義			
*糸/糹	jiǎo zì bù 絞字部	silk	zhǐ 紙	gěi 給	lěi 累
羊	yáng zì bù 羊字部	sheep	měi 美	qún 群	yì 義
老	lǎo zì bù 老字部	old	lǎo 老	kǎo 考	zhě 者
肉/月	ròu zì bù 肉字部	flesh	ròu 肉	dù 肚	féi 肥
艸	cǎo zì bù 草字部	grass	cǎo 草	huā 花	yīng 英
西	xī zì bù 西字部	west	xī 西	yào 要	fù 覆
衣/衤	yī zì bù 衣字部	clothing	yī 衣	zhuāng 裝	chū 初
*言	yán zì bù 言字部	speech	shuō 說	qǐng 請	xiè 謝
貝	bèi zì bù 貝字部	shell	mǎi 買	mài 賣	guì 貴
*足/𧾷	zú zì bù 足字部	foot	pǎo 跑	gēn 跟	lù 路
車	chē zì bù 車字部	vehicle	chē 車	qīng 輕	jiào 較
*辵/辶	zǒu zì bù 走字部	go, run	guò 過	zhè 這	dào 道

邑 (⻏)	yòu ěrduǒ 右耳朵	right ear	dōu 都	nà 那	bù 部
* 金	jīn zì bù 金字部	gold	qián 錢	qiān 鉛	zhōng 鐘
門	mén zì bù 門字部	door	wèn 問	kāi 開	jiān 間
阜 (⻖)	zuǒ ěrduǒ 左耳朵	left ear	yuàn 院	chú 除	yáng 陽
雨	yǔ zì bù 雨字部	rain	yǔ 雨	diàn 電	xuě 雪
頁	yè zì bù 頁字部	page	yè 頁	tóu 頭	yuàn 願
食	shí zì bù 食字部	food	shí 食	fàn 飯	è 餓
馬	mǎ zì bù 馬字部	horse	mǎ 馬	jià 駕	shǐ 駛
魚	yú zì bù 魚字部	fish	yú 魚	xiān 鮮	shā 鯊
鳥	niǎo zì bù 鳥字部	bird	niǎo 鳥	míng 鳴	fèng 鳳
麻	má zì bù 麻字部	hemp	má 麻	me 麼	huī 麾